I0748368

POUND ON!!

From the Glass Slipper
to the Glass Ceiling

Tales of Alpha Women Chasing the Fairytale

ROBIN ROTENBERG

ISBN: 978-0-578-70326-8 (paperback)
ISBN: 978-0-578-71253-6 (hardback)
eISBN: 978-0-578-70327-5

Published by Rotenberg Consulting, LLC

July 2020.

www.alphawomenrock.com

For my Mother

CONTENTS

CONTENTS

No one gave me a ladder; if there was one, no one told me about it. I had to climb the walls instead, and some days I truly felt like I was clawing at them just to stay in the same place. I couldn't look up or down for fear of falling, and I felt all alone, hanging on for dear life.

ROBIN ROTENBERG

INTRODUCTION

My Fairytale - How this Project Began

My decision to write this book collided with the TimesUp and MeToo Movements. I was planning my exit strategy from the corporate world where I'd notionally punched in over 30 years ago and had never punched out. It was time for me to move on, but every day the news was worse. Trusted men - actors, authors, broadcasters and others who were in my living room every day and in my favorite films were accused of heinous, abusive workplace crimes. I was shocked, disappointed and beyond betrayed. How could someone like Bill Cosby - America's model husband and father - be accused of drugging and assaulting women? How could someone like Harvey Weinstein assault and intimidate women in exchange for movie roles? More poignantly, how could they get away with it for so long? Why didn't anyone speak up? It made no sense to me, and rocked my world.

Instead of looking for answers where they would be impossible to comprehend, I decided to respond. Women, especially early in career women, need some positive stories about ordinary women in attainable careers as we chase our dreams. Not all men are monsters, yet not all career paths are smooth sailing either. They are, however, still very much worth pursuing. I had never before felt the need to talk about my experiences, or to showcase those of my other Alphas, but the time had definitely come.

This book is a pathfinder - a series of positive stories and guideposts to showcase Alpha Women who have overcome obstacles to chase our dreams. Our dreams are all different, but we each traded the fairytale of the glass slipper to chase some form of the glass ceiling. In the process, we pounded on that glass ceiling to try to break through and grab the brass ring.

I know all the Alpha Women in this book. Some I have known for decades, and others for a shorter time, but each one has taught me a lot and offered me a helping hand along my journey. Like the women themselves, their stories are motivating, inspiring, warm and funny. They are offered as a source of strength and hope for us all. My story is included here too.

Enjoy and learn. Let me know what you think at:

www.alphawomenrock.com.

A TIMELINE OF WOMEN'S RIGHTS

I am fascinated, and sometimes appalled, with women's treatment and rights in the United States and Canada. I am including a timeline of women's rights for both the United States and Canada as an overview of how far we have come, and how we got here. While we have a long way to go on our search for true equality, these milestones, achieved by courageous Alpha Women, give us hope that we are on the right track.

MILESTONES IN U.S. WOMEN'S HISTORY

1760

Men and women are one at law. [1]

The colonies adopt the English system of laws decreeing that women cannot own property in their name or keep their earnings. 1 and [2]

1777

All states pass laws taking away women's right to vote. [3]

1839

Married Women's Property Acts are passed by the States beginning in 1839. [4]

1848

Elizabeth Cady Stanton and four friends call a Women's Rights Convention and draft a "Declaration of Sentiments" at Seneca Falls, NY. [5]

1868

Congress passes the 14th Amendment to the Constitution, with "citizens" and "voters" defined as males in the Constitution. [6]

1869

Arabella Mansfield is granted admission to practice law in Iowa and becomes the first woman admitted to the legal profession in the United States. [7]

Wyoming, the Territory, grants women the right to vote in all elections. [8]

1870

Ratification of the 15th Amendment; African Americans can vote, but women, while not explicitly prohibited from voting, are not expressly guaranteed the right to vote either. [9]

Women start serving on juries in Wyoming. [10]

1873

Conviction of Susan B. Anthony, for "unlawful voting." [11]

The Supreme Court of the United States rules that a state can exclude a married woman (Myra Colby Bradwell) from practicing law. [12]

1874

The Supreme Court of the United States rules that women are "non-voting" citizens in Minor v. Happersett and that states remain free to grant or deny women the right to vote. [13]

1887

Susanna Madora Salter is the first woman elected Mayor of a town in Argonia, Kansas. [14]

1890

Wyoming is the first state to grant women the right to vote in state elections. [15] [16]

1900

By now, every state has legislation granting married women the right to keep their wages and to own property in their names. [17]

1916

Jeannette Rankin is the first woman elected to the House of Representatives (Montana). [18]

1918

Margaret Sanger wins her lawsuit in New York, thereby allowing doctors to advise married patients about birth control for health purposes. Her clinics later became Planned Parenthood. Sanger opened her first clinic in 1916. 18 and [19]

1920

The 19th Amendment, passed by Congress on June 4, 1919, is ratified on August 18, 1920, granting women the right to vote. [20]

1923

Alice Paul, suffrage leader, and attorney, initiates the campaign for the Equal Rights Amendment. [21]

1932

Hattie Wyatt Caraway of Arkansas becomes the first woman elected to the U.S. Senate. [22]

Frances Perkins, Labor Secretary, is the first woman to serve as a U.S. Presidential Cabinet Member. She was appointed Secretary of Labor under Franklin Delano Roosevelt. [23]

1934

Lettie Pate Whitehead Evans becomes one of the first female Directors of any major corporation when she is appointed to the Board of the Coca Cola Company. [24]

1936

Birth control is legal under medical direction under federal law and in all but a few states. [25]

1960

The Food and Drug Administration approves Enovid for contraceptive purposes for no more than two years at a time. [26]

1963

Betty Friedan publishes "the Feminine Mystique." [27]

The Equal Pay Act passes, prohibiting sex-based wage discrimination between men and women performing substantially similar jobs in the same establishment. [28]

1964

The Civil Rights Act passes, [29] which in Title VII bars discrimination in employment on the basis of race and sex. [30]

The Equal Employment Opportunity Commission (EEOC) is established to investigate complaints and impose penalties. [31]

1965

The United States Supreme Court overturns a Connecticut law prohibiting the use of contraceptives by married couples. [32]

1968

The EEOC rules that sex-segregated help wanted ads in newspapers are illegal. [33]

1969

California adopts the nation's first "no-fault" divorce law, allowing divorce by mutual consent. [34]

Shirley Chisholm of New York becomes the first African American woman in Congress. (She was elected in 1968, and was inaugurated in 1969). [35]

1971

The Supreme Court of the United States rules that Marietta Corporation cannot refuse to hire women with preschool-aged children while hiring men with preschool-aged children.

The Civil Rights Act 1964 requires uniform minimal qualifications for males and females unless there is a reason to differentiate based on business necessity. [36]

1972

The Equal Rights Amendment is passed by Congress and sent to the states for ratification, but dies in 1982 since it is not ratified by the 38 state minimum. [37]

Title IX of the Education Act prohibits sex discrimination in education programs that receive federal support. [38]

The Supreme Court of the United States upholds the right of married couples to use birth control. [39]

Juanita Kreps becomes the first woman director of the New York Stock Exchange. [40]

1973

The United States Supreme Court decides in Roe v. Wade that women have autonomy over their pregnancy during the first trimester. [41]

1974

Congress outlaws housing discrimination based on sex. [42][43]

Cleveland Board of Education v. LaFleur declares it illegal to force pregnant women to take maternity leave. [44]

U.S. TIMELINE CONTINUED

POUND ON!!

1976
Nebraska enacts the first marital rape law. [45]

1978
Title VII of the Civil Rights Act of 1964 passes, prohibiting sex discrimination on the basis of pregnancy. [46]

1980
Paula Hawkins becomes the first woman elected to the U.S. Senate without following her father or husband into the job. [47][48]

1981
Sandra Day O'Connor is appointed as the first female United States Supreme Court Justice. [49]

1983
Dr. Sally K. Ride becomes the first American woman to be sent into space. [50]

1984
Geraldine Ferraro becomes the first woman nominated Vice President on a major party ticket. [51]

1986
The Supreme Court of the United States holds that a work environment can be declared hostile or abusive as a result of sexual harassment. [52]

1992
1992 is declared Year of the Woman after the 1991 Anita Hill/Clarence Thomas hearings. [53][54]

1994
The Violence Against Women Act passes, tightening federal penalties for sex offenders, and providing for specialized training of police officers. [55]

1996
Ruth Bader Ginsburg writes her landmark decision in U.S. v. Virginia stating that the Virginia Military Institute could not refuse to admit women.[56]

1997
Madeleine Albright becomes the first woman Secretary of State. [57]

2005
Condoleezza Rice becomes the first African American female Secretary of State. [58]

2007
Nancy Pelosi becomes the first woman Speaker of the House. [59]

2008
Sarah Palin becomes the first woman to run for Vice President on the Republican ticket. [60]

2013
The ban against women in military combat positions is removed. [61]

2016
Hillary Rodham Clinton is the first woman to lead (as a Presidential candidate) the ticket of a major political party. [62]

As of January 2, 2016, women can serve in any job in the armed forces that meets gender-neutral performance standards. [63][64]

2017
Congress has a record number of women. 105 women hold Congressional seats - 21 in the Senate and 84 in the House of Representatives. [65]

The Women's March is organized to advocate for women's rights. Upwards of 3 million people turn out, marking one of the most massive and peaceful protests in U.S. history. [66]

MILESTONES IN CANADIAN WOMEN'S HISTORY

1756 - 1866

With few exceptions to the colonies that would later form Canada, the vote is a privilege reserved for limited segments of the population, mainly men. [1]

1849

Harriet Tubman, born a slave in Maryland, escapes. She leads many other slaves to freedom by helping them escape to Canada through the Underground Railroad network. Tubman remained a suffragette until her death in 1913. [2]

1851

Mary Ann Shadd Cary, born in 1823 as a free American black woman, emigrated to Canada in 1851, where she opened a school for the children of fugitives. [3]

1853

Mary Ann Shadd Cary becomes the first black woman in North America to found a weekly newspaper - The Provincial Freedom. She later returned to the U.S., where she became one of only two black women ever to have cast a vote in a U.S. Federal Election. [4]

1859

Upper Canada allows married women to own property, but not to sell it without the agreement of their husbands. [5]

1875

Grace Annie Lockhart graduates Mount Allison University with the first university degree awarded to a woman. [6]

Dr. Jennie Trout returns from an American medical school with a degree. She is the first woman licensed to practice medicine in Canada. [7]

1885

In Alberta, unmarried women property owners are granted the right to vote and can hold office in school matters. [8]

POUND ON!!

1892

The Law Society of Upper Canada gains discretionary power to admit women as solicitors. [9]

1897

Clara Brett Martin becomes the first woman lawyer in the British Empire after having challenged the Law Society of Upper Canada. [9], [10]

1903

Emma Sophia Baker is one of the first two women to earn a Ph.D. from the University of Toronto. [11]

1909

The Criminal Code of Canada is amended to criminalize the abduction of women. Similar penalties had already existed for stealing cattle. [12][13][14]

1916

Manitoba, Saskatchewan, and Alberta give women the right to vote and hold office. Manitoba is first. [15][16][17]

Emily Murphy is appointed Canada's first female magistrate (judge) and is the first female police magistrate in the British Empire.[18]

1917

Roberta Macadams and Louse McKinney become the first women members of a Legislative Assembly (Alberta). [19]

1918

With some exceptions, the Canada Elections Act gives all women over 21 the federal vote. (Some provinces followed later). [20]

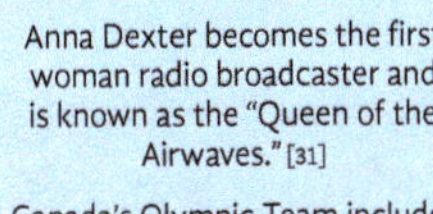

1919

Women in New Brunswick get the right to vote in provincial elections. [21]

Helen Armstrong, as the President of the Winnipeg Women's Labour League, is a leader of the Winnipeg General Strike in which 30,000 striking workers shut the city down.[22] [23]

1921

British Columbia passes maternity leave legislation, becoming the first province to provide maternity leave for working women. [25]

Agnes MacPhail becomes the first elected woman member of the Federal Parliament (the House of Commons) by campaigning for prison reform, old-age pensions, and gender equity, among other things. [26] [27]

1922

Some women in Prince Edward Island win the right to vote in provincial elections. [28]

1925

Federal Divorce Law changes allow a woman to divorce her husband on similar grounds to those under which a man could divorce his wife. [29]

Mary Irene Parlby becomes the first female Cabinet Minister in Alberta. [30]

1921 - 1926

Nellie McClung becomes the Liberal member of the Alberta Legislature for Edmonton. [24]

1928

Anna Dexter becomes the first woman radio broadcaster and is known as the "Queen of the Airwaves." [31]

Canada's Olympic Team includes women for the first time. [31]

1929

The Judicial Committee of the Privy Council (JCPC) overturns a Supreme Court of Canada case to the contrary, and declares women to be "persons" and therefore eligible to hold the office of Senate in Canada. [31,] [32]

1940

Women gain the right to vote and run for office in Quebec elections. [33]

1942

Eileen Tallman Sufrin organized the first Canadian bank strike in Montreal. [34]

1948 - 1949

Asian women gain the right to vote in Federal Elections. [35]

1951

Ontario is the first province to put equal pay legislation into effect. [36]

1957

Ellen Louks Fairclough becomes the first woman Cabinet Minister, as Secretary of State under Prime Minister John Diefenbaker. [37]

1960

Aboriginal women (and men) are granted the right to vote in Federal Elections. [38]

1964

Bill 16 passes in Quebec, giving married women the same rights as their husbands. [39]

1969

The Federal Government decriminalizes contraception and allows abortion under certain circumstances. [40] [41]

1971

Amendments to the Canada Labour Code establish a 15-week maternity leave. [42]

1972

Rosemary Brown is the first black woman in Canada elected to a Legislature. [43]

1974

Pauline Jewett becomes the first woman president of a co-ed University (Simon Fraser). [44]

The first female RCMP recruits for regular police duties begin training in Regina, Saskatchewan. [45] [46]

CANADIAN TIMELINE CONTINUED

1980

Alexa McDonough becomes the first woman to be elected leader of a provincial party (the Federal New Democratic Party) while holding a seat in the Legislature. [47]

Jeanne-Mathilde Sauvé becomes the first woman Speaker of the House of Commons.[48]

1982

The Canadian Charter of Rights and Freedoms is enacted, including s.15, the Equality Clause. [49]

Bertha Wilson is the first woman justice to serve on the Supreme Court of Canada. [50][51]

1983

The Criminal Code of Canada is amended to allow spouses to charge each other with sexual assault. [52]

The Canadian Human Rights Act prohibits sexual harassment in workplaces that fall under Federal jurisdiction. [53]

1984

The Right Honourable Jeanne Sauvé becomes the first woman Governor-General of Canada. [54]

1985

Indigenous women are permitted to retain their Indian status even if they marry non-status men. [55]

1988

The Supreme Court of Canada strikes down Canada's abortion law as unconstitutional. [56]

1989

Audrey McLaughlin becomes the first woman to lead a national political party.[57]

The Canadian Human Rights Tribunal rules that obstacles to military jobs must be removed for women (with a few exceptions). [58]

1993

Kim Campbell becomes Canada's first female Prime Minister. [59]

2000

Beverly McLachlin is appointed Chief Justice of the Supreme Court of Canada. [60]

2004

Louise Charron is the first native-born Franco-Ontarian to serve as a Supreme Court of Canada judge. [61]

Rosalie Abella is the first Jewish woman to sit on the Supreme Court of Canada. [62][63]

2005

Michaelle Jean is the first Afro-Caribbean Governor-General.[64][65]

2006

Bev Busson is the first woman commander of the Royal Canadian Mounted Police. [66]

2009

Andrea Horwath is the first woman leader of the Ontario New Democratic Party. [67]

2010

Kathy Dunderdale is sworn in as the first female premier of Newfoundland and Labrador.[68]

2013

Kathleen Wynne becomes the first female Premier of Ontario and is the first openly gay premier in Canada.[69][70]

2015

The Federal Election saw 88 women winning seats in the 338 member House of Commons, a gain of 12 seats over the previous record of 76 women elected in the previous Parliament.[71]

The Government of Canada announces a fully gender-balanced Cabinet consisting of 15 women and 15 men, the first gender-equal Cabinet in Canadian history.[72]

2017

Saskatchewan passes legislation providing protected leave for victims of domestic violence. [73]

2017

Millions globally participate in women's marches and rallies to call for a more inclusive, equitable, and just society for all. [74]

WHAT IS AN ALPHA WOMAN?

Becoming Alpha

The concept of an Alpha Woman is somewhat revolutionary and evolutionary at the same time. In today's world, Alphas are trailblazers, leaders of the pack who drive change and make our own rules. The term "Alpha" was not initially used to describe a woman, as it was intended to connote a leader rather than a follower, a dominant and determined being who would fight undeterred toward the goal of survival i.e. an Alpha Male or other animal. Referring to women as Alphas is a revolutionary concept. With original roles of support (Beta or Omegas), we were gatherers rather than hunters; submissive followers. The characteristics of Alphas in common parlance referred to Alpha males, or Alpha dogs or other "top" animals. Times, however, have changed, as have archetypes, role models and stereotypes. Here is what an Alpha woman may look like today, as divided into 5 Categories or Phases on the Rotenberg Axis (Figure 1).

First and foremost, it is important to remember that Alpha Women evolve. We are not born in the end state of a super charged Alpha Woman, knowing the ropes & sharing war stories. We start out more starry-eyed and naïve than that, not knowing what awaits us as we commence our climb toward the glass ceiling. Once we abandon the glass slipper dream and chase a different fairytale, we start out with certain qualities and characteristics which evolve through various phases and stages.

While there may be some overlap along the climb, I would fit the Alpha characteristics into 4 main stages of development or phases, with a 5th Stage of "Absolutely Alpha" where the Alpha has truly arrived, with some traits being more dominant than others at any given phase. They are: Attempting Alpha (Phase 1), Learning Alpha (Phase 2), the Professional Alpha (Phase 3), the Hard Driving Alpha (Phase 4), and the Absolutely Alpha (who rocks!) (Phase 5).

Not all Alphas will have every characteristic, and any of these qualities may ebb and flow throughout our careers. It is very likely that women along our career paths will possess qualities from each Phase at any given time. What is important is the desire to succeed and improve, to learn and grow continuously along the way, and to help one another both celebrate success and learn from opportunities as we go.

Just as a side note - the first initials of all of our Phases spell the word "ALPHA"...Attempting, Learning, Professional, Hard Driving, and Absolutely Alpha.

ATTEMPTING ALPHA
Phase 1 of our Evolution

The Attempting Alpha is our colleague, sister, aunt, mother, daughter or friend who is beginning her journey. In this first phase she will be very AMBITIOUS with HIGH ASPIRATIONS and a very strong desire to succeed. She's hungry for success and DREAMS BIG. The Attempting Alpha must be AGILE, able to switch gears quickly, and to grasp concepts or understand situations with relative ease. There are different kinds of agility, and the Attempting Alpha must show signs of them all in some way - intellectual, people and change agility, for example, so she can navigate all the obstacles being thrown in her path. Similarly, her DETERMINATION must be unflinching and resolute. Otherwise the Attempting Alpha will be thrown off course easily and may stray from her dreams and goals. It is difficult to be determined and stay that way, but stay that way she must.

CURIOSITY may have "killed the cat", but it is a necessity of life for the Attempting Alpha woman. A strong desire to learn and inquire is essential to Alpha growth, especially now. This spirit of INQUISITIVENESS will evolve over time, but will stay with her and fuel her drive forever. Moral PRINCIPLES and STRONG ETHICS are essential for the Attempting Alpha who will encounter many people along the way who do not share this quality. She must use her unimpeachable ETHICAL grounding to evaluate her path right from the start. Straying and short cuts are the easy way out; having ethics and INTEGRITY are a strong and critical differentiator for any Alpha.

LEARNING ALPHA
Phase 2 of our Evolution

As the Alpha evolves, her CREATIVE ideas begin to shine through. Her IMAGINATION and ORIGINAL IDEAS are essential to her recognition and ascent. Being INNOVATIVE and having ORIGINALITY separate the Learning Alpha from the rest of the pack. Feelings of CONFIDENCE and SELF-ASSURANCE are similarly indispensable for a Learning Alpha. She must learn to appear POISED and COOLHEADED in the face of any challenge. She can never let them see her sweat!

The INTELLIGENCE of a Phase 2 Alpha begins to shine brightly through the maze of early obstacles and challenges. ASTUTE, INTUITIVE thinking starts to show and differentiate her from others. This DISCERNING NATURE will serve her well, especially when combined with an ELOQUENT and ARTICULATE speaking style. Being articulate helps Learning Alphas persuade others and state her goals and aspirations clearly and definitively. She will have to learn it if it is not innate. The ability to ASSERT herself is an important differentiator as well. She must always say what she wants. No one will ADVOCATE for you as well as you can advocate for yourself!

PROFESSIONAL ALPHA

Phase 3 of our Continuous Evolution

Alphas must remain UNDETERRED along the way, and keep her LION-HEARTED DAREDEVIL nature alive. COURAGE is a daily requirement for a Professional Alpha who by now has several years of TENACITY under her belt. To others she may appear BOLD and DARING, to her this is her mantra coupled with her firm and constant LOYALTY. Our Professional Alpha remains FAITHFUL and true to those who have helped her get this far. She needs her community and strong SOCIAL ties since the collective is of penultimate importance to her. She must still put herself in others' shoes (Manolo's or Louboutin's, of course!), able to understand and share the feelings of those around her. This high EMPATHY will be needed to feed her success and drive her brand. It also compels others to follow her example, and to respect her as she is RESPECTFUL of others.

HARD-DRIVING ALPHA
Phase 4

The Hard-Driving Alpha is a powerhouse AUTHENTIC woman whom others lean on and APPROACH for advice and good counsel. She is the real deal with nothing fake or spurious about her (except maybe a few eyelashes), with a GENUINENESS which is palpable and TRUSTED. Unlike others in so many ways, her trademark WELCOMING disposition draws others to follow her like the Pied Piper. While DEVOTED to her career and those important to her, she demonstrates an admirable DEDICATION to causes, people and places to which and whom she is inseparably CONNECTED. She is RESOLUTE in her staunch INTEGRITY and can be relied upon in that regard. While not afraid to show her VULNERABLE side, her weaknesses do not hold her back. Her incredible GIVING NATURE can compensate for challenges and showcase GENEROSITY and KINDNESS. Never perfect, but always striving to do better, the Hard-Driving Alpha is universally sought after and admired.

ABSOLUTELY ALPHA

SHE ROCKS !! - Phase 5

The Absolutely Alpha woman is a fabulous mix of all characteristics of the other earlier categories. Through continuous improvement and self-awareness she has demonstrated HIGH PERFORMANCE and HIGH EMPATHY. She recognizes and is recognized for her strength and determination, and is a sought after mentor, speaker, teacher and advocate. The Absolutely Alpha has learned to balance all aspects of her life of greatest meaning to her, giving 100% of her presence to family, friends and colleagues when called upon to do so.

She understands that just showing up matters, and that what you say to others has impact. Above all else she is a mature contributor who has endured many challenges to achieve her success. On any given day she will exhibit many Alpha qualities, giving back to her community and those around her. She is fastidious when choosing confidantes, and while always striving for more, she is grateful for what she has achieved. Her positive stories of her attainable career serve to inspire and motivate others. She rocks!

THE ROTENBERG AXIS AND HOW TO USE IT

Figures 1 and 2 are an assessment tool for determining where we are in our Alpha journey. Alphas are asked to choose up to 10 characteristics which describe herself at the time she is using the Axis.

The x axis represents IQ, and the y axis represents EQ, or emotional quotient characteristics. Each of the Alpha quadrants sets out characteristics of that Alpha Phase. For each of the Phases, the characteristics are assigned points.

The characteristics in Quadrant 1, or the lower left quadrant represent the earliest characteristics displayed by a developing Alpha Woman. She is agile, ambitious, determined, curious and ethical. These traits are visible early and are essential to Alpha development.

So far, she has lower confidence and is building her skills. Each of the traits in Quadrant 1 is assigned 1 point.

In Quadrant 2, the Alpha has progressed along the more intellectual traits, showing herself to be creative, confident, intelligent, articulate and assertive. She is starting to have career success, but is not as developed on the empathy side. If any of these traits are chosen, they are each assigned 2 points.

Quadrants 3 and 4 represent higher Alpha characteristics which emerge when the EQ and the IQ are more evident in the climb. Quadrant 3, or the top left quadrant, showcases more ruling characteristics. The Alpha Woman is becoming move involved with those around her, and is courageous, loyal, social, empathetic and respectful. Each of these traits is assigned 5 points.

Quadrant 4 represents both extremely high intellect and high emotional intelligence. This Alpha Woman is authentic, approachable, dedicated, vulnerable and generous. Each trait is awarded 10 points.

To use the Rotenberg Axis, the Alpha chooses up to 10 characteristics which best describe her at the time. She then tallies the points assigned to each trait to find her Alpha Score. The Scores are as follows:

0 - 10 Points - Attempting Alpha

11-25 Points - Learning Alpha

26-40 Points - Professional Alpha

41-50 Points - Hard-Driving Alpha

51 Points or more - Absolutely Alpha

Once she has determined her Alpha category, the participant can purchase our Tip Sheets for each Alpha Score if desired. See alphawomenrock.com for details.

Alpha levels can vary greatly depending on your then current circumstances, and will change and evolve over your career and life. It would not be unusual for an Alpha to toggle between the various Alpha Phases as she ascends, given career and life changes. The important thing is to continue the climb, and always attempt to ascend to the Absolutely Alpha Phase where you have learned much and have great positive lessons to share.

POUND ON!!

FIGURE 1

Rotenberg Axis
BECOMING ALPHA

FIND YOUR ALPHA SCORE

0-10 Points
Attempting Alpha

11-25 Points
Learning Alpha

26-40 Points
Professional Alpha

41-50 Points
Hard-Driving Alpha

51 Points or More
Absolutely Alpha

The Rotenberg Axis

FIGURE 2

WHAT DOES YOUR ALPHA SCORE MEAN?

0-10 Points
Attempting Alpha

11-25 Points
Learning Alpha

26-40 Points
Professional Alpha

41-50 Points
Hard-Driving Alpha

51 Points or More
Absolutely Alpha
SHE ROCKS!

Rotenberg Axis
ALPHA QUADRANTS

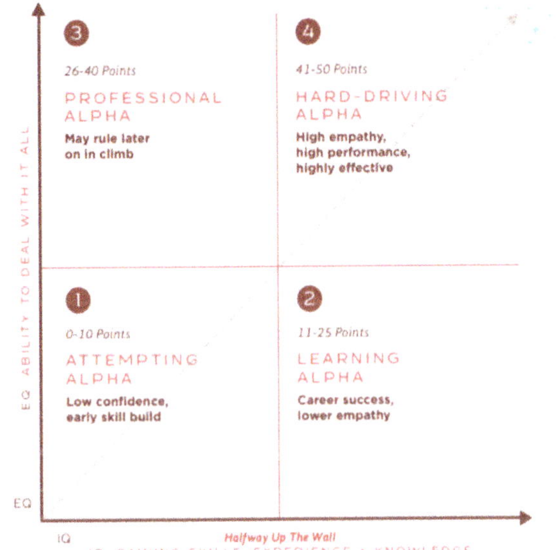

POUND ON

INTERVIEW QUESTIONS FOR ALPHAS

To provide a preview of what you can expect in the pages ahead, I'm sharing the interview questions sent to each of the Alphas in the early phases of developing this book.

BACKGROUND QUESTIONS

- Describe your early life. Where did you grow up, and with whom? Who were your friends? What sorts of activities and sports did you participate in? Where did you vacation with your family? Etc.
- With whom did you spend most of your time with growing up? How do you believe they might have influenced you?
- What was your favorite subject in school? In which subjects did you excel? In which subjects were you challenged?
- Where did you receive your education and what was your focus? What was the most important thing you learned during your education?
- Were there women you admired growing up? If so, who were they, and why?

CAREER BACKGROUND

- Did you choose your career, or did it choose you? Tell us about your career progression and what you learned from each step.
- How did you develop your most utilized skills? Are there skills you wish you had developed further?
- Did you have mentors? If so, who were they, and what did you learn from them?
- Did you receive any memorable feedback? If so, what did you gain from it?
- What challenges did you face as a woman leader? How did you rise to meet them?
- What is the biggest compliment you ever have received regarding your leadership? Your career?

CURRENT LIFE

- Describe your life now. Where do you live? With whom do you live? Who in your circle of family, friends, and professionals, do you spend the most time with? Do you have any pets?
- What do you like to do to relax?
- What is your current job and what do you love most about it?

POUND ON

- Describe your typical workday.
- How would you describe yourself as a leader? How might others describe you?
- How has your career affected your relationships, both past and present?
- Describe your typical weekend.
- What is it you might like to do next in both your personal life and career?
- Are you working toward a legacy? If so, what does that look like for you?

INTROSPECTIVE:

- Who do you think has had the most influence on you overall?
- Who or what inspires you today? In particular, which women leaders inspire you today?
- What accomplishments are you most proud of, in both your personal life and in your career?
- What do you believe have been the keys to your success? What does success look like to you?
- Where do you believe you have failed? What did you learn

from your biggest mistake?

- What do you think makes a good leader?
- What does balance mean to you and how do you pursue it?
- What do you know now that you wish you had known when you started out?

IDEALS:

- How might leadership be different for women than it is for men?
- Name three things a woman leader must do to succeed. Would these same three things be required of a man? Why or why not?
- Do you believe it is easier for working women today than it is when you first started? Why or why not?
- What three pieces of advice would you give to young working women today?
- What three pieces of advice would you give to young women in middle school, high school, and/or college today?
- What is one thing younger women still need to remember (or learn) about the gender gap today?
- What are some steps we need to take today in order to

continue narrowing the gender and pay gaps?

- Do you feel women unfairly bear the "mental load," and if so, do you have any ideas of how to adjust the scale?
- What do you think women's leadership will look like in ten years? What do you hope it looks like?
- Do you think women can "have it all?" Why or why not?
- What traits, in your opinion, define an "alpha woman?"

YOUR FAVORITES:

Please list your "favorites" and give brief reasons as to why:

- Vacation Destinations (both visited and wanting to visit)
- Foods (dessert counts)
- Artists (of all mediums)
- Music (singers, bands, Broadway, composers)
- Books (or authors)
- Sports/Exercise (which you play, watch, or support)
- Hobbies
- Movies
- Television Shows
- Mobile apps (what has made your life simpler?)

ROBIN ROTENBERG

Glass Slippers and Steel Stilettos

POUND ON!!

ROBIN ROTENBERG

My Story - Glass Slippers and Steel Stilettos

At this point in my life and career, I often have young women and men seeking my advice and counsel. This always surprises me; I feel like I have very little to offer them. I always thought I'd come in every day and work hard, and that that would be enough. I couldn't have been more wrong. I never thought myself worthy of recognition or greater opportunity. It shocked me when I was selected for executive C-suite jobs. Any recognition by peers or other women was a surprise to me too. In hindsight, I see that I was different, that I had a different drive and ambition, different work standards, as well as different ideas about success and what it looked like to me.

I never intended to be a trailblazer. I simply went into work every day working hard at everything I was handed to do. While this may not be the story of every woman who puts her head down and perseveres, I believe that this very work ethic led me to greater opportunities and aspirations, including researching and writing my own book.

In crafting the introduction to this book and reflecting on my past, I thought back on what a tremendous influence my family had on me. One lesson in particular stands out: Be proud of how you behave. The strong women who came before me taught me that lesson, and with this book and with every day of my life, I continue to honor their memory by making every day count.

I grew up in a peaceful, safe and over-protected suburb of Toronto Canada. I am the eldest of two daughters, born to a housewife and an economist. My father wanted a boy but claimed repeatedly that he was just as happy when he learned I was a girl. I have always doubted that.

Both of my parents and three out of my four grandparents were college educated. My father was a brilliant student, finishing high school at 16 and earning a Masters Degree in Economics before he was 21 years old. My mother had a degree in General Arts, with a focus on Art History, and loved the arts. Like the rest of my family they had gone to the University of Toronto. My paternal grandmother, my Grandma Tessie, was a very strong influence on me, and had also excelled academically. Unlike most women of her time, she had attended university. She not only attended, she had earned a Masters in Applied Math. While she was permitted to excel academically, her mother didn't like it if she played sports, considering it unladylike. My Grandma Tessie used to tell me that she had to lie to her mother when she came home with red cheeks after playing basketball after school. Rather than tell her mother she was playing a sport, she told her instead that the wind had reddened her cheeks. This had a profound effect on her; she always encouraged me to pursue whatever activities I wished and to be proud of it. In terms of her life, she married a wealthy Toronto businessman who owned properties and had an insurance company. I never knew my paternal grandfather Charles; I am named in his memory (my middle name is Charlotte). They gave my father, their eldest child, what looked to me like a charmed, privileged life. He and his siblings, a brother Harvey and a sister Leila, grew up in a wealthy Toronto area. Their families had been in Canada for several generations, were university educated, and extremely successful.

I saw my Grandma Tessie once a month for dinner at a fancy restaurant. As a child I thought she was strong and powerful, capable of anything. I still do. She must have thought so too. She even ran the insurance business and their apartment buildings after my grandfather died. I have always felt that she was way ahead of her time. Her strength and liberal ideas were truly remarkable for a woman born in the early 1900's. In spite of her toughness, my Grandmother had a good heart. She told me that she didn't raise the rents of her tenant families who couldn't afford to pay because she didn't think it was right. She also advocated for me to my parents who were very overprotective. I once wanted to go to a school dance when I was 12 or 13 and my parents wouldn't let me go saying that I was too young, and that I would be out too late. I called my Grandmother who asked a few questions about what the activity was, and declared that I should be allowed to attend. It was my first successful negotiation. I learned early to figure out who was on my side, and to use it to my full advantage.

My mother Bonnie was the middle of three siblings, and had an older sister Evelyn and a younger brother (also) Harvey. She grew up in a nice area, much less affluent than that of my father's family. My maternal grandparents were Russian immigrants who came to Canada at the turn of the 20th century to avoid religious persecution. They came to the country as small children and lived in an immigrant "ghetto" area. My maternal grandfather (also Charles), known to us as Grandaddy, was very entrepreneurial, and had worked in danger climbing the city trains to earn money for his university tuition. He graduated as a dentist in the 1920's, after having been expelled with 11 of the 12 Jewish students and thereafter reinstated with the help of the organization B'Nai Brith. He recounted this story to me several times during my childhood, as it had had a strong effect on his identity and security. Grandaddy was always suspicious of people, and worried that they were somehow going to harm him if they could. He really struggled as a young dentist. The economy in the 1920's was tough, and he had a lot of trouble getting paid by his patients. Grandaddy told me that a patient once paid him in chickens. I have vivid childhood memories of him making collection calls to try to get paid. This left its mark on me as well. I wanted to make sure I worked for people or companies who could pay me. It just didn't seem right that Grandaddy would work so hard, do a good job, and not get paid for the work. I've always carried a bit of that insecurity as well, never being sure that I can count on anyone or anything to take care of my needs.

Grandaddy was also an inventor. He worried a lot about the radiation from x-rays. In his early days as a dentist there was a lot of radiation exposure from the equipment. After suffering with skin cancer on his hands from taking dental x-rays, Grandaddy developed several radiation-blocking devices like lead aprons which he sold to large companies. I don't think he made much money from all his inventions, but he wrote papers and kept developing protective devices. I was the model for his promotional brochures and I remember posing for pictures wearing weird headgear or aprons from the time that I was 4 or 5 years old.

My maternal grandmother, Jeannette (known to us as Grandma Jeannie) always claimed that she was born in Toronto rather than Russia and that her passport was incorrect. She also said her age was wrong, and that she was much younger than her documents said. Grandma Jeannie was eccentric in other ways as well, and while a style icon she only wore the color purple. She said other colors washed her out. In fact, her whole house was decorated in purple, as was Grandaddy's dental office including his dental chair. Grandma Jeannie was the only one of my grandparents who was not formally educated, since she had to go to work to support herself when she was only a teenager. Grandaddy, however, trained her to be his dental hygienist and surgical nurse. Grandma Jeannie insisted on being paid for her work and opened her own bank accounts to save her money, a lot of which she spent on me and my sister. As a young woman, Jeannie was a milliner and had owned a store with her sisters selling hats, gloves and makeup before her siblings moved to California. Her siblings had a store in Watts, California which had been burned down in the riots of the 60's. We talked about that a lot in my household; how unfair it was that they lost their livelihood to violence. I could not understand that kind of hatred. I still don't.

While profoundly deaf, Grandma Jeannie never let on, reading lips and carrying on conversations that didn't reveal her challenges. In her 80's she taught herself to type so she could contact us through the newly created hearing-impaired phone operator. Grandma Jeannie also collected antiques which I thought were junk. She said she wanted her children to have nice things, so she shopped and stored a lot of silver, china and home goods in their home and basement. It was all junk to me, but treasures to her. That junk now represents my treasured memories of my Grandma Jeannie, along with her teachings about makeup, hair, nails, fashion and independence.

My childhood summers were spent at summer camps in a Northern Ontario, Canada provincial park where I made lifelong friends, learned to sail, canoe, horseback ride, smoke, kiss boys and many other things not fit for print. Mostly, I learned independence and how to fend for myself. After my initial feelings of abandonment for having been sent away, I felt free. Freer than I have ever felt before or since, which is odd since I was actually trapped at camp in the middle of a forest with no way out. I learned how to take care of myself, portage a canoe, build a campfire and safely put it out, and how to avoid conflicts with the mean girls, of which there were many.

My first experiences with the mean girls were at camp as a ten-year-old, which created in me bewildering feelings of exclusion and failure. It was the first time that social experiences were negative for me. I'd always had lots of friends in my neighborhood, and gotten along with all of them. The mean girls I encountered at summer camp were very different than the other children I had known, and formed groups or clicks of girls who were "in" or "out". Being the nerdy smart girl coupled with being very shy did not earn me a spot in the clicks of the "in" crowd. In fact, I was excluded from all the cool social happenings, and left to feel isolated. I found other friends who were more similar to me, experiencing the same exclusion. I also learned strength of character and to choose friends wisely; a lifelong hard-taught lesson.

Camp was my first job. I became a Camp Counselor as a teenager, and spent my summers working at camp until I was in University. I returned summer after summer to the comfort and safety of old friends and familiar wild surroundings. Lying out on a dock at night staring at the summer stars to the rhythm of lapping lake water brought me a peace and calm I had never known. I still feel that way about stars and water. Not about the camping – now I only camp in 5-star hotels!

During the school year, I was always over-programmed with dance and music lessons, swimming, skiing (I was horrible at it) shows and concerts. I was always very busy as a child, and didn't have much time outside my various activities. I believe that it was my mother's goal for me to be competent at many sports and activities, many of which I still pursue to this day. Her love of the arts was also passed to me. She started taking us to children's concerts and ballets as small children which instilled in me a true appreciation for those with talent. The Nutcracker and Toronto Symphony Orchestra childrens' concerts are very happy memories for me.

Of course, there was family and food – not necessarily in that order. I spent Friday nights and Sundays with my maternal grandparents. Grandma Jeannie would cook all week for us and send home food with my mother every Friday night. My mother, while beautiful, was a lousy cook. My father said he had to buy a rotisserie for the oven when they were first married so that he wouldn't starve. There were holiday parties with cousins and friends, a Yacht club where we went on weekends when I wasn't shipped off somewhere, and lots and lots of schoolwork. I knew early on that school was very important and that I too was expected to go to University. Even though I wasn't a boy.

Life continued into my teenage years, and seemed pretty good, at least from the outside. My mother had a deep adoration for prescription drugs, especially valium, and my father suffered with bouts of depression. I was quite oblivious to these problems at the time, and was more concerned with my activities, school work and the few close friends that I'd developed.

My life changed radically when I was 15. During that year both my mother and my Grandma Tessie died. Their deaths tore our family apart and sent me into a tailspin. I learned grief and sadness far too early. I also learned about perseverance, inspiration and honor. I vowed to live my dreams, inspired by the women who had gone before me, and to appreciate every day. During this unimaginably tough time, I sought ways to honor the role models I had lost, hoping that I would never feel worse than I did during that time. I learned perspective, and to view career and other setbacks in their proper place. I think that these early losses taught me to look at life with gratitude and perspective. I still try to keep a good balance and not take things too seriously. As long as my feet hit the floor and I can brush my own teeth, I know it's a good day.

After my mother and my Grandma Tessie died, I plastered a smile on my face and carried on, aware that I was different than the other teenagers, and eventually throwing myself into school. I understood that other children had the support of their families, and was painfully aware that this would be pretty much lacking in my life going forward. Certain family members who were not fond of my father started excluding us from the celebrations we had always attended. While I don't have high inclusion needs, being ignored after a lifetime of inclusion in family celebrations really hurt. Like dealing with the mean girls, I started forging my own path and developing my own relationships. I also knew that an education was my ticket out, and a means to finding recognition and value. I was good at it, at least on the languages and arts side, and I had teachers who took an interest and encouraged me. School became both my validation and salvation. I didn't realize it at the time, but a good education would also provide economic freedom;

with a good education I could get good jobs and not have to rely on anyone who might abandon me.

When the time came for me to apply to Universities, I applied to a few – none of them where my family wanted me to go. I was expected to go to the University of Toronto like all my family members before me. I didn't apply there, and I got accepted into every other school where I applied. My father initially refused to pay my tuition, so I got a job and off I went, leaving my family members shocked at my steadfast independence and my determination to think for myself. My father eventually relented and helped me out, proudly telling me that I could become anything I wanted to be, and that he would help me. I think he just didn't know what else to do, but I am grateful for the support he offered.

Leaving home was the best thing I ever did and was the first of many decisions I made in defiance of or in contradiction to the advice of others. These decisions were mine, and mine alone, and I had no intention of letting anyone else make them for me. I never quite trusted that anyone else had my best interests at heart. While listening carefully and considering the consequences, I made the very important decision of where to go to school based on what I thought was right for me, not the wishes or desires of other people, even my father. I never looked back, and I have carried the motto of making my own decisions with me throughout my life. I make decisions based on what I think is right at the time, not on what other people think is right for me. Even if my decisions are wrong, at least I will have made them myself.

In the end, I earned three University degrees from two different universities, neither of them the University of Toronto. I did take a summer school course there one year, which made me even more sure that I'd made the right decision to go somewhere else.

My degrees were in studies of my choice, again in defiance of and in contradiction to the advice or desires of others. I had no real advisors or counselors, so I made my decisions on my own with a little help from my friends. My high school and Universities offered no meaningful counsel either, so I was really left on my own to decide what to study. I earned degrees in Political Science, Education with an emphasis on special needs children, and a law degree. A good basic foundation for a girl from the Toronto suburbs to find a job and support herself.

I taught special education for a year, which surprised no one, but wasn't enough for me. It was also fraught with bureaucracy and government administration. Many of the families didn't have the means to get the help their children needed, and I had to help them apply for government funding in order to provide appropriate educational tools for the students. I found this very frustrating, but it led me to advocate for the children and their parents, which was one of the reasons I decided to return to school.

Although I loved my students and stayed in touch with many of them for years after I taught them, I thought I could do more. I'd always secretly dreamt of being a lawyer – it was impressive and sounded so glamorous. I could also do more for children and their families than I could in the bureaucratic maze of the education system, so I applied to law school. There are no lawyers in my family. There are lots of architects, designers, artists and medical professionals. I had no one to rely on to ask about the practice of law, but I applied and went anyway despite the opposition of family and friends. My ongoing independence continued to lead me to forge my own path.

University was the first place where I figured out that I'd had a nice upbringing, and that I'd had lots of options that other girls didn't have. Some girls I met had to pay their own way through school, even though their brothers didn't. I felt that this was really unfair and I didn't understand it at all. Didn't women have a right to an education and to earn a living? How could we achieve equality and have independence without a good education? It was one thing for my father to refuse to pay initially because I wouldn't go where he wanted me to, but I was learning that other girls were disadvantaged in their families simply because of their gender. The reality horrified me.

In law school I started realizing that men and women did not have the same career options. Less than 1/3rd of the class was women, which surprised me. I didn't understand why it wasn't at least 50%. We women students seemed to win a lot of the awards and were just as dedicated to the law as the men. My eyes were starting to open wide to the issues of gender and career opportunities. At least the female professors were activists, who inspired me to learn about women's rights and how the court system treated women. Some areas of law regarding women's rights were so antiquated that I had a hard time believing it. Systemic discrimination continued to open my eyes as I saw how important it is to find our voices and use them. I learned the importance of speaking up, not just for myself but for others. Most importantly I learned to speak up for injustice and for what I believed in. I loved the study of law and worked hard to be recognized and to achieve.

My first legal job was with a big Bay Street law firm. I learned a lot from the senior lawyers who gave good advice about ethics and taught me practical skills. In other ways, working for a big Bay Street law firm tested my naïveté. The few women lawyers didn't help each other, were highly competitive and worked incessantly. I questioned why they hired overachievers with lots of outside interests, and then took away all of our free time. At the time there were no real mentoring programs, so we young lawyers had to figure it out on our own. In addition to the legal advice from skilled advocates, I got a lot of unsolicited advice from the secretaries who were the gatekeepers to the senior partners. For example, the secretaries told me to cut my long hair and take off my red nail polish, neither of which I did. They also didn't like my earrings (I wore 5), which I continued to wear. I didn't see how changing those things would make me a better lawyer. Clients with little filter on how they behaved repeatedly asked me if was old enough to do the job, and wanted to take me out to dinner. Although I loved the work, I started to question whether I was strong enough to withstand the pressure to perform and conform, the bureaucracy, and the unwieldy clients. I was looking for a guidepost and for encouragement, or at least a good role model. Not finding it, I instead honed my people skills, grew an even tougher skin, and soldiered on.

I admired many women during those early days, but they were all in virtually unattainable careers. Heads of state, performers, movie stars, journalists, singers and dancers. I looked for their common traits and tried to figure out how I could be like them even without their talent and fame. I saw that they thought for themselves, made their own decisions, took on meaningful work, and most particularly they earned their own money. My father always told me to learn to type so that I wouldn't starve. For his time, he was right. I had no intention of starving, but I intended to do a lot more than type for my career.

I started to figure out that women had to behave much differently than men to succeed, which seemed patently unfair, but was the grim reality. I was spending a lot of time proving that I had a brain, and an equal, if not greater amount of time, hiding it from the people who couldn't handle it. I'm smart, but no rocket scientist; I just work really hard with what I have. Another lesson from my Grandaddy. I couldn't figure out why my being smart was scary to others, but that's what I was repeatedly told. How could an early in career lawyer be so smart she scared the clients and partners? I think it was more that people underestimated me and were surprised that I could think. It made no sense to me but made me feel like an excluded outsider; somewhat like how I felt with the mean girls at camp, although now the stakes were higher. I had rent to pay, and I'd spent years of effort to get there.

I felt like I had to conform to succeed, which for me was somewhat counterintuitive. I had fought hard to get where I was, defying the views and opinions of others, and refusing to conform. I didn't think I should have to conform and be like everyone else for my contribution to be valued. For women to succeed we need to find our voice, use it without apology, and speak up when we have a point of view. This does not mean that we have to think like everyone else, or hide our views or intelligence from others who can't handle it, both men and women alike.

Over the years I have developed many self-taught rules around finding my voice and using it. While difficult at first, I have learned that using my voice is a strong differentiator and provides a role model to others. If we just sit back and take it, we can be seen to acquiesce. If we acquiesce we are accepting how others treat us, which will only perpetuate existing systemic problems. No matter how much opposition is in the room, my hard fought rule is to speak up within the first ten minutes of a meeting if at all possible. That way I can find my voice early on, making it easier to continue to do so. It also shows attendees that I intend to participate not just watch, and that I expect to be heard and my contribution to be respected, even if it is rejected.

I went from a large law firm to a smaller one, hoping to get more interesting work and have a better life balance. The work was fundamentally better; if the senior partners were unavailable for court attendances I got to go in their place. For me, this was incredibly rewarding; to have an audience in front of the Ontario

Court of Appeal as a young lawyer was truly a dream come true. Back at the office I found similar issues around proving myself, being heard and having a voice. This seems to be a constant theme for women in professional positions which I have continued to hear over the years. The issue of women not helping each other has also continued. It would be a long time before I saw any change in that, watching it happen with the advent of women's organizations which I was initially reluctant to join for fear of being singled out rather than accepted.

The fact that women didn't help one another left an indelible mark on me. I vowed to change that in my career wherever I could, and to always help promising young women coming up behind me. I continue to do that by making time, no matter how little, to spend with earlier in career women who want to have coffee or are seeking a little advice. It doesn't take much to make a big and memorable difference to others.

I was learning that in order to succeed I needed to keep my confidence high and develop a high and healthy self-awareness and self-evaluation system. Not getting much validation from others, nor feedback whether it be positive or negative, I developed my own performance rating system which I still use to this day. I evaluate my performance at the end of every day and after every meeting. What could I have done better? What did I learn? I have always kept a running list of improvement opportunities to make sure that I continuously do better.

Time marched on, as did my career. I had gotten married (for the first time) soon after university, and my daughter Taryn was born while I was practicing law at the smaller firm. As a mother, my career became even harder to pursue, as did proving my capability and credibility. I took nearly a year off when Taryn was born, which was unheard of in those days, being told that I would sacrifice my career. I did it anyway. When Taryn was almost a year old I rejoined the workforce with a company, rather than staying at the law firm. I moved to a part-time in-house legal job, so that I could supposedly have better life balance. New computer technology allowed me to take the work home, which turned out to be both a blessing and a curse. I was still working all the time. While grateful for the opportunity and truly loving the work, I still found myself struggling for recognition and acceptance, never confident that my contributions were valued. I worried every day whether I'd have a job the next. I think some of that insecurity was borne from watching Grandaddy's struggle to get paid. I felt I had no one to help me if I was in need, which also creates different concerns than if you have a strong family behind you. Necessity is the mother of invention.

The Corporate world was a whole new experience for me, offering different kinds of opportunities and challenges alike. Having worked in a law firm surrounded by other lawyers, I was suddenly thrust into a world full of engineers, scientists, sales people and marketing professionals. It was a different world, and one which I found perplexing and mesmerizing at the same time. In a law firm you hang up the phone or shut your office door and your clients are gone; you don't live with them and confront them all day long. In a corporation it is much different; you have only one client and they are in your face constantly. While the closeness allowed me to give better advice, it also meant that I was much more vulnerable to not having a job if my client became displeased. This placed many different pressures on me as an in-house lawyer.

I have always enjoyed the creativity of being in a Company. This creativity allowed me to try to prove myself in different ways.

As a result, I found myself in a position of being the first woman in many situations – the first General Counsel, first to be on the Management Team, first to Chair the Pension Committee, the first woman President, and later the first woman Chief Communications Officer. Like being the firstborn, I felt a tremendous responsibility to live up to the expectations of my bosses, as well as the weight of responsibility to other women. I felt like any failure on my part would be seen as theirs as well, and that I would be letting everyone down if I couldn't do my job to a high level of excellence. I once had a boss say to me as I took on a new assignment "Failure is not an option". No pressure there.

In the early days, I worked part-time in the office, but until all hours of the night at home. I wanted to keep my part-time status, perform to a very high standard, and still have time with my daughter. My feelings of responsibility to other women weighed on me as well, and compelled me to work judiciously remotely so no one complained that I wasn't physically present. Teleworking was virtually unknown at that time, and it was unusual to be out of the office unless you were traveling on business. Hence, I felt like an experiment that had to succeed.

Being the first at anything puts you under a microscope, and I was told that repeatedly. I knew that I was closely watched, and that I carried a big burden. If I failed, it would be a very long time before other women were offered the same opportunities and I knew it. I had never intended to trailblaze. I just went in to work every day and worked hard at everything I did. The fact that it led me into great opportunities was just a coincidence, I felt. These feelings of responsibility have never left me. I just try to use them to energize myself to aim higher and do better.

I have tried to ignore the burden of trailblazing and enjoy the ascent and the view, knowing that I would have to continue to climb the walls and hang on tight. Forget about a corporate ladder – I was too busy trying not to slip and fall or land on a mine-field to look for one. I always try to be proud of how I behave – a lesson from my Grandma Jeannie – and another one of my rules. "You have to look in the mirror and face yourself every day", she would say. "If it doesn't feel right, don't do it", I was told by an admirable senior partner at my first law firm. Good guiding principles as I was starting to figure out that not all people behaved like I did. I have always wished I'd learned that sooner.

I recall a management meeting discussing a new dress code proposal where I was not only the sole woman at the table, but a different generation than the men. The discussion degenerated, and I received a few insults which I didn't appreciate. I later marched into the offender's office and demanded a public apology. He apologized privately, but I told him that wasn't enough; he couldn't insult me publicly and try to apologize within the safe closed-door confines of his office. Today I would have spoken up right away in order to be true to myself and follow my "speaking up" rule. In any event, I got my public apology at the next management meeting.

It is also important to be true to oneself. Whatever your values, wishes and dreams, they are yours alone and should not be compromised for anyone else. Otherwise, it will be impossible to look at ourselves in the mirror. I had a key chain that had the Shakespearean quote "To thine own self be true" which I'd picked up along the way. I carried it around for years until it broke, but still carry that message in my head every day. There are lots of opportunities to compromise our principles. Don't do it.

My first leadership roles involved administrative assistants, and it wasn't until later that I supervised managers. Supervising administrative assistants can be challenging if they don't have the skills or they have a lousy work ethic, but they are expecting you to direct them which in some ways makes it easier. I learned the hard way to set the expectation that my assistants keep my private information private, and not talk about me to the rest of my department. I was unpleasantly surprised early on by some assistants who spent more time chatting around the office than working, and needed to be reminded that they were there to get work done and not create a soap opera environment where there are layers of social acceptance. There are no mean girls in my department, at least not for long.

Expectations for women bosses are different; there is a level of friendship expected that does not seem to be expected from men. It is a tricky balance between being their boss and keeping a bit of distance, and being friendly enough to have a pleasant working relationship. The best assistants don't want or need your friendship, but others are resentful when they don't get it.

Leading managers is harder still, and setting expectations early on is invaluable. Managers are an entirely different type of worker and pose many challenges for their leader. While this appears the same for men, for women it can be even harder, especially if the male workers resent having a woman boss. In one role I had to supervise managers who had been promised my job. It was very difficult to try to win them over, and some never came around. I had to make difficult decisions and move people around, including exiting a few. It was tough, but I couldn't risk having unmotivated disloyal employees. That would not have been fair to me, to the other employees, or to the company that was paying our salaries. I was amazed at the daring entitlement that some of the employees had; why did they think they were owed something by the company? It is an employment relationship; you have to do your job in order to keep it and get paid. While new in the role, I drew on my fierce tenacity to lead, but it was no easy task.

Women's leadership is different than a man's. Women walk a fine line between directing and mandating, and we have to be careful how we deliver advice. If we appear too pushy we are admonished for being nasty and too direct. If we are too polite we are seen as soft and easily intimidated. It's important to remain true to our own personalities, and not change how we act simply because others are trying to get us to be different than our true selves. On the other hand, we have to appear professional, tough and capable, which can look different to different people. We also need to establish our own brands; mine is to always be extremely well-groomed, the best dressed and the best prepared, no matter what the work occasion. Confidence is built from the inside out; we have to feel it in order to convey it. Even though our employees want autonomy, when the going gets rough they look to their bosses for direction and advice. I once confronted a situation where a very sick employee had to be wheeled out of a rest room by ambulance attendants. She had just returned after a lengthy illness, which she'd obviously not conquered. I was very upset, having been the one who assisted her when she fell ill, and afterward I showed it. I was surprised how much that had affected my staff; they must have always expected me to be strong but emotionless. When I showed emotion they were even more upset about their sick colleague, and talked about my reaction for days. It was a big lesson to me about showing my humanity more often. My colleagues shouldn't have been so surprised by my reaction when a sick colleague was wheeled out of the office on a stretcher.

POUND ON!!

I'd had my credibility questioned for so long as a young professional that it took some coaching to push me along as a strong, authentic and connected leader. It took a while for me to understand that people needed to trust me to follow my lead and to deliver beyond the bare minimum. I made the mistake of seeming too aloof at the beginning; my shyness from the mean girl experience made me hang back. I didn't have the awareness at the time to realize that this was preventing my larger team from performing to their highest potential. Around that time, 360 feedback was coming into vogue, as were leadership retreats which were focused on team building. As part of the feedback I solicited responses from my direct reports. I was shocked to learn that I was seen as cold and aloof. My direct reports wanted to know me better, and I was told that this lack of knowledge of "who I was" prevented them from fully trusting me and delivering at their highest levels. I have since worked hard to show my genuine warmth and empathy without seeming soft. In particular, I talk to people more and share some personal information. A delicate balance, but one that's attainable.

My initial foray into leadership had a hard and turbulent landing. Aside from the issues with my direct reports, I found that people didn't work like I did, and they didn't have the same goals and ambitions. That was a very tough lesson for me. When the clock struck 4, it was like a fire alarm for some workers. Out they ran, with no intention of doing anything work related until the following day. It took me a long time to adjust to that, and to find consistently hard workers to work with me. I also learned to accept that not everyone wanted or needed a career like mine, and that was ok. I was very surprised the first time I offered a promotion to someone and they turned it down. They liked their job, their lifestyle, and had no ambition or desire to do anything different or tasks which were more challenging. It has taken me a long time to accept that, but I now do.

Leadership is a lot like being a mother. You have to know and understand the capabilities of your children, strive to bring out the best in everyone, and never (or almost never) give up. I learned that the defeats or shortcomings of others were neither mine nor mine to fix, but this took time. While warming up and becoming more approachable, these were still work relationships and I had to keep up a certain barrier. Leaders at work are not meant to solve everyone's problems or even talk about them. While I need to be aware of team members' capabilities, I am not their mother, partner, sister, aunt or friend. To this day, I remain circumspect about what I ask and what I share. I just don't think that my co-workers need to know the most intimate details of my life, and frankly, I don't want to know theirs. We all need to leave things at the door and come in to work and work hard every day. This can actually be very helpful when things are tough personally. Work can be a safe place to hide from personal problems at times; I've used it that way throughout my career when I have had the need to throw myself into my work to find validation or salvation. Kind of like how I threw myself into school after my mother and Grandma Tessie died when I was a teenager.

I think the most important thing about being a good leader is being consistent. Your employees, colleagues and bosses should know that you have the maturity to come in every day and behave appropriately. Even if things go wrong you have to show a demonstrated capability to find your way to a good solution. As a leader, your employees should know they can always come to you when things go wrong; that you are approachable and won't blow their heads off. I once had a boss in a law firm who threw the furniture around his office when he got mad. We could hear it from the adjoining offices. It certainly didn't make us want to go ask him for help or deliver bad news. We all have our bad days, but we still have to show up as strong leaders who can cope. As I often say to my leadership team, "Be careful how you behave today. The first thing your employees will talk about around the dinner table tonight will be about you – their boss. What do you want them to say?".

It is equally important not to talk about people behind their backs, especially your boss. I have a rule that I don't say anything behind someone's back that I wouldn't say to their face. I might say it differently, but the message would be the same. Also, I rarely forward my boss's emails. I need to trust my bosses and have them trust me, and private conversations should remain that way, even in writing. It's important to treat people with dignity and respect, and that includes what you say about them when they're not there, or what you do with their information and correspondence. Be careful what you say about others. They will invariably find out, so you might as well find a way to say it to their face in the first place.

Emails travel easily and can get you into a lot of trouble if you're not careful. We can be far too lax with our written correspondence, and let it become too casual. It is dangerous to forget that emails at work are company property, and could land in a court case if an issue is contentious. Pretend your boss is looking over your shoulder before you hit the "send" button, or imagine that your notes might end up in front of a judge. That way, you will pause to reflect before you send something that can be potentially problematic. On the topic of gossip, be careful what you say about others.

I hope people would say that I am an honest, consistent and fair leader. I certainly try to be that way. I give a lot of thought to how I treat people, and carefully consider all options before making a decision that will affect someone's career or life. Fairness and justice are very important to me and are big reasons why I went to law school. I just think there isn't enough justice in the world; maybe I can add my little bit to make the world better. At the same time, I also want people to see me as a tough leader and negotiator. One of the greatest compliments I received early on was from a schoolmate on the other side of a difficult case. The case was very contentious, and involved disputed facts and a lot of money. Neither client wanted to go to court, so we reached what I thought was a good compromise. My colleague on the other side later said that he'd settled the matter because I was such a tough negotiator that he took what he could get and closed the file. His comments were early confirmation to me that I could be seen as an equal - tough, fair, yet feminine - and still win.

I have found that negotiating, like leadership, is different for men than women. It is easy to be underestimated, which makes others think they can take advantage. Social norms and mores teach young girls to be nice and get along; that's what we all heard from our mothers. It was not, however, what I heard from my Grandmothers who taught me to fight hard and not worry so much about being "nice". We have to move away from the social expectations of being "good", test our mettle and bargain for all we're worth. We must repeatedly prove ourselves for others to trust our strength and tenacity.

Through my own experiences I've seen that women also have to fight harder to be taken seriously. I always found it aggravating to be underestimated or treated like I'm an idiot.

Underestimate me at your peril, I would think to myself, but it's a disadvantage all the same. If we're underestimated, it's hard for people to take chances on us for jobs and other opportunities. Letting others believe I'm a fool might be advantageous during a negotiation, but it still makes me mad. I don't want to set that as the norm for women coming up behind me and have them think that they have to look weak to succeed.

When I first started working there were no formal mentoring programs like there are now. In fact, there was very little informal mentoring happening either, especially among women. Most women made it their business not to mentor other women, and said so quite openly. I've never had a mentor per se, but I've had some bosses who have taken chances on me and sponsored me. Since I've largely kept my head down and worked hard, I've been surprised at being identified for bigger opportunities. The fact that I've been considered always flattered me, since I know I wouldn't have been on a candidate slate unless others had confidence in my ability. My bosses also knew I didn't shy away from change, and that I embraced a new challenge even if it scared me to death. Good practices, albeit somewhat frightening. I always expressed gratitude for the new opportunities, and I hope I never let them see that I took on the new challenges with a bit of fear.

As a leader, I have often seen people fail because they get the question wrong. It is very important to get the question right in any task we are tackling. Over the years I've seen people expend a lot of time and effort answering the wrong questions, which is a total waste of energy. It only takes a few minutes at the outset to ask a few questions to define the task. We don't do it because we are afraid of looking stupid or incompetent. I think it's better to clarify the question at the beginning than wasting a lot of time and looking incompetent later on.

I always ask my team about the atmosphere in a meeting, what will/did the room feel like? It's important to feel the room and adjust your tone and material to fit it. It's like walking into a courtroom. You need to listen to the judge before you start talking. If they got up on the wrong side of the bed that morning you'd better get straight to the point, get what you want, and get out fast. Similarly, if the atmosphere is warm and inviting you should embrace it, enjoy the conversation and savor the moment. Successful dialogue is a very enjoyable part of our careers and we should appreciate it.

Leadership is also about demanding respect, both for and from your team. Another one of my rules is not to take any crap from anyone, and I've learned that others are more than willing to try giving out a lot of it to mask their insecurities. Along with fairness and justice we need respect, otherwise workplaces degenerate into playgrounds with untempered mean bullies. You won't keep your good people very long in situations like that.

I feel very grateful for my life, my family and my career. I have found and seized a lot of opportunities thanks to a great start and an emphasis on education, hard work, justice and fairness. I hope that is my legacy. Whenever an early in career woman thanks me for something I have done for them, I ask them to remember it so that they can someday do the same for someone else.

It is important to "pay it forward" and treat others with the kindness and respect we have benefited from ourselves. That way we can achieve lasting, enduring change for women in our families, workplaces and societies. I have seen a lot of change in women and women's leadership over the years, and I hope we continue to grow and evolve. There are many attainable careers that women can have if we educate ourselves, pursue our dreams and aim high.

Hard work and perseverance really do pay off. We must continue to Pound On!! the glass ceiling so we can bust through and grab the brass ring!

POUND ON!!

Pictured: Grandma Jeannie and Granddaddy on vacation in the 1960's.

Pictured: My mother on her wedding day, May 14, 1953.

Pictured: My parents and my Grandma Tessie, on the couch in my Aunt Leila's house, circa 1953.

Pictured: My parents, my sister Wendy and I, on the same couch in my Aunt Leila's house, circa 1966.

Pictured: Taryn at age 3, circa 1996.

Pictured: My daughter Taryn walking me down the "aisle" on my wedding day, August 3, 2008.

Mitch and I on our wedding day, August 3, 2008

Pictured: My husband Mitch and I at my daughter's Bat Mitzvah, November

Pictured: Taryn and Carter dressed up for Halloween 2017.

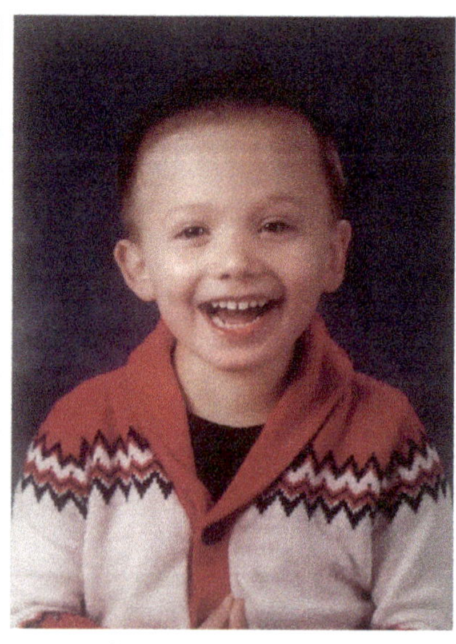

Pictured: Carter's School Picture 2019.

IRENE CHANG BRITT

Born in Taiwan and raised in the suburbs of Toronto, Irene Chang Britt's Alpha traits were visible early when she started a business with her brother while she was still a student. Warm and welcoming, Irene's keen business acumen led her to great corporate success where she ran a Fortune 500 Company as CEO. Now a member of several Boards of Directors, Irene continues to use her fine skills to drive top flight business results for the companies she serves.

Irene earned a Bachelor of Arts in Social Anthropology from the University of Toronto, and an MBA from the University of Western Ontario.

POUND ON!!

IRENE CHANG BRITT

An Incredible Alpha Success Story

From my first corporate assignment in 1986 to the portfolio of brands I currently serve as Board Director and Chairperson, I am known for leading turnarounds, fixing what is broken, and transforming businesses. I love solving problems, even if I'm told they can't be solved, but this takes personal resilience and a lot of tenacity. Let me tell you how I got here.

My wonderful childhood began in Taiwan, where I was born the youngest of 4 siblings - I have sisters who are older than me (10 years and 7 years respectively), and a brother who is 4 years older than me. My parents moved to Taiwan in 1948, just before the Communists took over China. Living in a democratic society was very important to them; I think they were truly remarkable for how strongly they held these values, and for the life they wanted to give us. They were really brilliant people, and I admired their great work ethic and success.

My mother was an only child, and was thrust into war and poverty in China with my grandmother after my grandfather passed away suddenly. My grandmother worked hard at menial jobs to send my mother to school, and years later, she became a successful administrator. My dad was one of 10 children, and was a very successful economist. They both spoke many languages fluently. Their hard work and educations allowed them to enjoy success in Taiwan and to have a good life there.

In 1964, when I was just 18 months old, my parents decided to move us to North America, once again seeking out a more democratic society, sacrificing their own comfort for the sake of their children's future. The six of us, and my maternal grandmother, left Taiwan and moved to North America. We moved to San Francisco first, and eventually settled in a lovely suburb of Toronto. I think a lot about the sacrifices my parents made for us; moving to Canada in their 40s with 4 young children, leaving everything behind to have a better life.

We were always a very close family. We talked about politics, history and democracy around the dinner table a lot when I was growing up, and we lived by that example. We vote in every election, and are very grateful for our rights and freedoms. We never take them for granted, and always try to give back. We have always stuck together as well, knowing that we needed each other's support and guidance as immigrants to the country.

Our experiences as a family led me to study social cultural anthropology at the University of Toronto, but even before that I had a lot of entrepreneurial spirit. While I was still in high school, my brother and I opened two stores and a mail-order business for high-end European style bicycles. We were both competitive cyclists at the time, and we decided to go into business together, starting up the company with a lot of elbow grease, plus money I'd earned teaching English to new immigrants. We learned a lot through trial and (lots of) error, and this led me to go for an MBA at Western's Business School. My business experience, and some gentle prodding from my mother to get a "practical" education had encouraged me to apply.

The hard-learned lessons from our cycling business followed me into business school, where I continued to learn about business, but also about fitting in. As an Anthropology Major and bike shop owner, I showed up to our MBA orientation in bike shorts, which was my uniform at the time. I was the only student not wearing a suit, which was not a great feeling. I felt really out of place, and went home crying, worrying that I'd never succeed in that academic environment. I did manage to work my way through the first semester, but I technically failed the semester and was told to consider dropping out. I was so disheartened that I considered it. Fortunately for me, when one of my professors learned I wanted to quit he challenged me to continue, calling me a "chicken". This only inspired me to fight back and set my sights on doing well. I didn't know it at the time, but he told me later that I reminded him of his wife who was a real fighter, and was then fighting breast cancer. He knew that I would fight back if he challenged me. He was proud, but not surprised, when I made the Dean's List 2 years later. That professor had a really strong influence on me, and was one of the first people who saw that I had potential.

I met my husband Tony in business school. In class one day, I asked the woman sitting in front of me to explain something related to accounting because I had no idea what they were talking about. She said she didn't know either, and suggested I ask the student sitting beside her. It was Tony. He turned around, and I knew right away that this was the guy I was going to marry. When he proposed 2 weeks later I asked him what had taken him so long! He told me that he knew right away as well. We are still an incredible match that started as love at first sight.

Tony has always had a profound influence on me, largely because he sees things in me that I don't see myself. I was very intimidated in business school until Tony reminded me that I was a successful business person already, not just a successful student like many of the others in class. This was really an epiphany for me, and really helped me see myself differently. Tony has always given me tips on how to succeed, especially about not being so deferential. He is basically charming and irreverent, but has a great sense of self which helps him follow his own views and form his own opinions. His influence has helped me immensely to overcome my inherently introverted nature, and has allowed me to swim against the tide in business as well. I have really learned a great deal from Tony and how he approaches the world, and I am very grateful to him for his support.

When I was in my first year of business school and looking for internships, I had the chance to meet the Vice President of Sales and Marketing in Canada for Kimberly Clark (KC), the paper goods manufacturer of brands such as Huggies and Kleenex. When he learned that I'd owned my own bike stores and knew the sports retail industry, he mentioned that they'd just bought a running insole company and that they needed someone to start the business in Canada. What serendipity! Was I "interested", he asked? Of course I was, even though he just made the job up on the spot! I later accepted a job in sales and marketing at KC because I liked the people, even though I'd been offered "shinier" jobs. Accepting the job with KC was one of the best decisions I've ever made - I ended up staying with Kimberly Clark for 13 years. Taking the job at KC in its industrial unit rather than in consumer brand management of Oreo at Nabisco, taught me that it's not always best to grab the shiniest object. The most interesting things tend to be "dull" on the surface , as they are puzzles that need solving and can generate great opportunities.

I've learned a lot of lessons along the way, and one of them is about balance. I've learned that you are never truly balanced on any given day. You have to look at the big picture and ask whether you are happy with the choices that you've made. I count on that. For example, when Tony and I were home with our kids, we were always present, both in body and in mind. Nothing distracted us. When we found that two careers in sales and marketing were too much and we couldn't juggle it, Tony decided to stay home to run our household. This was truly amazing. He did a lot of volunteer work and fundraising, and looked after everything else. With my husband at home, I had other lessons to learn. One was that I needed to let go a little bit. I had to stop worrying about the small stuff, i.e. whether there were socks on the floor. I had to learn not to be a perfectionist and hurt myself with my own standards.

As my son and daughter grew up I continued to take on different business challenges, including working my way up to SVP and President, North America Foodservice at Campbell Soup Company. Never wanting to let "a good crisis go to waste" in 2008, at the beginning of the Great Recession, my team and I devised a breakthrough strategy to totally disrupt the industry, and we doubled the profitability of the unit in short order. This required a lot of tenacity and resilience, and I am happy that it worked. I have learned to take these kinds of chances, take risks, and drive change.

Another key learning is that you have to push back when someone is hurting you. At one point earlier in my career, I was running a $1b business in a company. My male colleague was running a $300 million business in the same entity. Although he was running a smaller business, he was always trying to use his male collegial relationships to freeze me out. One time, he succeeded in disinviting me to a business discussion by relocating it to a strip club. That was quite the effort, just to try to gain the advantage! When I suggested that the venue was inappropriate, another male colleague suggested I was being too sensitive. This was very disappointing to me, but I refused to let them diminish my voice and demanded that we meet an hour earlier the following morning to start our meetings. This was an early lesson in how people (notably a man in this case) were trying to exclude me from the business discussions by capitalizing on relationships with male peers. Women need to learn from this sort of bravado too, but it really speaks to inclusion. It's crucial to bring your whole self to work, and for colleagues and bosses to respect your voice and viewpoint. Otherwise the workplace is hard to tolerate.

If I were giving advice to a woman earlier in her career, I would tell her that networking IS working. It's very important to carve out time for networking and to build relationships. You learn so much by just talking to other people. Women need to build relationships in business, and to understand how important these relationships are to our careers. I often observed men walking around the office with their coffee cups at 5:00 p.m. chatting with others and networking. We women remained at our desks and kept working, which we thought would help us get ahead. We were wrong. We thought we could get just as far by working hard, but it's not true. We have to take the time to build relationships which will accelerate our careers. We also need to tout our accomplishments and those of our teams. We have to be our own advocates, and talk about our great work. Otherwise, others will not know or understand what we achieve.

Similarly, don't stay with a company that doesn't understand your worth. I once told a boss that "I love this company, and I respect you. But never, ever confuse that with me needing you all." I truly believe that we have to know our worth and not feel beholden to anyone. We have to take charge of our own careers, compensation and futures.

I learned early on in my expertise of turnarounds and transformations that "who is on the bus" is the most important factor, and that trimming your team of people who actively work against a strategy is critical and urgent. While difficult, it's best to find these things out early on, deal with them, and form a team that believes in the new direction. I have also learned that women need to help each other. I try to give back, and still mentor and coach many women to help advance their careers. My husband and I have the goal of establishing scholarships for students of color who might not be able to afford college.

I wish I'd known earlier on that mistakes are ok. You have to make them and learn from them too. I feel like I was always fighting for respect; something that followed me into the business world from our childhood dinner table being the youngest of 4 siblings. Being overshadowed sitting at that dinner table with brilliant siblings and parents is a feeling that I've carried with me. I never wanted to be told that I didn't know what I was doing in business, even though my thinking is not linear and my desired future state results might seem far-fetched. I've learned that it's important to listen, and would emphasize this skill to earlier in career women as well. It's a very important skill to share. Share your skills, best practices and learn from others too. Brush off the things that "hurt". If something hurts you or you argue with others, try to move past it and keep on pushing. We are taught as young girls to care and to be nice. That's fine, but that's only half of the formula. We also need to have the arguments "on the field" or in the boardroom and then go out for lunch or a drink and let them go. My daughter, who was a field hockey goalie, is really good at that. Playing team sports has helped her know to fight on the field and then drop it. It's a good lesson. Similarly, little things, like connecting, matter. When I was retiring from my CEO position I received hundreds of emails from well-wishers. The one that resonated with me most was from a man on the production line in one of the bakeries who wrote to tell me that he appreciated how

I always remembered to ask how his daughter was doing. She was not in good health, and it meant a lot to him that I remembered to ask him about it when I saw him at the site. His note moved me to tears.

Over the past 15 years I have really made a strong effort to help others; to reach down and pull up. I feel so fortunate to have had such tremendous success through good luck and hard work. I feel that it is my obligation to help other women and people of color, and I try very hard to do that. I invest in women's issues and issues for people of color. I know that some women climb the ladder and then pull it up behind them so no one else can climb up. I think that is wrong. I once had a CEO from a large oil and gas company offer me a position on her Board even though I was from a different industry. This was a very powerful lesson for me - she wanted to help me rise, and the opportunity truly helped secure my career. It helped catapult my career, both in the C-Suite and in the boardroom.

Today I serve as Board Director and/or Chairperson for 5 boards. I'm proud that I've become a "growth-oriented catalyst" having turned around businesses that have been bleeding cash, and made them successful. I've ripped apart stagnating businesses to make them thrive again. I love to solve those kinds of problems, even in my own life! I love to constantly be in motion. When I'm not helping businesses grow, I'm either deep into Tai Chi or Qigong, or taking a long walk after cooking in our kitchen, or traveling. Standing still is not my style.

Pictured: Irene and her husband Tony

POUND ON!!

LYNDA COVELLO

Photo by Peggy Lampotang

A talented musician, artist, author and lawyer, Lynda blazed her trail in the big city of Toronto, far from her remote childhood home of Thunder Bay.

Lynda's entrepreneurial Alpha Woman risk-taking led her to big Bay Street law firms, her own Intellectual Property practice, and in-house to corporations where she has negotiated complex international agreements to fully leverage her clients' rights and earning potential.

Incredibly talented, Lynda performs in jazz clubs, paints, writes novels and other works, and trains with her horse. The first university graduate in her family, Lynda earned a B.A. (Specialist International Relations) from the University of Toronto, and an LL.B and LL.M (Jurisprudence) from Osgoode Hall Law School at York University.

POUND ON!!

LYNDA COVELLO

Dreams of Space, Deep Sea, and Freedom

When I was younger, I gravitated toward men's conversations at large family gatherings because I often found them more interesting. Though I never was invited to participate, I discovered that if I made myself small and kept quiet, eventually, I was ignored and could eavesdrop on the conversation. Men talked about the world and what was happening in it. I loved to listen in. A woman's world seemed so small and confined to me, filled with nothing but recipes, housekeeping tips and children.

It wasn't until many years later that I realized that these women actually were the backbone of our family. Some of them were college educated, a rarity in that time and place, and many were even teachers. They believed in themselves when others did not, worked harder than they thought they ever could, and shattered societal expectations.

I exist because many women in my family and their feminist male partners dared to break the "rules," to cross cultural, religious, familial and geographical barriers to be together on the north shore of Lake Superior, where I was born. They were uprooted, displaced, abandoned and disinherited, yet they persisted and even prospered. They fought for the right to be accepted, educated and to love who they loved – rights people are still fighting for today – and, while none of them are written about in history books, when I think about their lives and stories, I am inspired.

My paternal grandmother, for example, was a teacher educated by the church and on her way to becoming a nun. My grandfather changed all that, after emigrating from southern Italy to Port Arthur, Ontario at the age of 13 to work with his father at the rail yards. When he and my grandmother met, she defied the Roman Catholic church to pursue a life with him, and together, they became a cultural force in their town. Though they faced prejudice and opposition, as Italians still were considered second-class citizens in those days, they were undeterred in building a family and a community around music, education and community service.

My maternal grandparents also emigrated to Canada. Though my grandmother was born in 1903 in Indiana, when her father died when she was three years old my great-grandmother remarried and relocated the family to Canada. Oddly enough, though she never lived in the U.S. again, my grandmother still always identified herself as American. She worked as a secretary and office manager before marrying (and when I got married, was the only one in my family to support me in my decision to keep my maiden name) and also survived a number of near drownings in her life, in both Indiana due to floodwaters and in Ontario due to a boating accident. She was determined to survive and was a real fighter.

Sometime in the 1920s, my maternal grandmother met my grandfather, who had come to Canada from the Scottish Highlands to search for his older brother, despite being disinherited by his traditional farming family for doing so (we later learned his brother had also been in a boating accident and drowned). My grandfather found work as a prospector, staking mining claims in northwestern Ontario, before meeting my grandmother at a community dance.

After they were married, my grandmother would move herself and their five children from camp to camp, giving birth in rough surroundings without medical facilities and keeping everyone alive despite a myriad of dangers from the vast stretches of boreal forest. My grandfather was often gone for months at a time, with my grandmother rarely having any idea of where he was. Eventually, she put her foot down and insisted they move to Port Arthur, where she believed their children would get a better education. My grandmother taught me that you must endure whatever life throws at you until you figure out how to survive. She also taught me the only person that you truly can rely on in life is yourself.

My mother was raised as a Scottish Presbyterian, and my father as an Italian Roman Catholic. When they met in high school, they belonged to worlds that were not supposed to "mix." Still, they fell for each other and never looked back. Nothing was going to keep them apart and, after more than sixty years, they are still together.

My mother insisted on completing her nursing degree before marrying my father, even though he made it clear he intended to support her financially. She continued to work as a nurse until the birth of her third child and held jobs as a retail business owner and tribunal adjudicator afterward. Intelligent, practical and creative, she taught me self-discipline and crisis management skills that continue to serve me well to this day.

My father worked full-time in the family business, a recreation center, from the time he graduated high school. When the city expropriated the center's property for urban renewal in the early 1970s, he was 36 years old, had little formal education and had four children to support. He and my mother looked at various options, including moving our family to Hawaii, where the demand for Canadian nurses was high thanks to their good training. However, around the same time, my father became friends with a man who ran the Canadian division of a multinational corporation in England (and whose son I would eventually marry). He offered my dad a job at the Thunder Bay branch of his company. This was an industry my father knew nothing about, so when he accepted the job offer, he insisted on starting from the bottom as a warehouseman rather than in sales. Eventually, he moved up the ranks to become a manager of the northwestern Ontario district and exponentially increased sales.

I grew up in Thunder Bay, Ontario with my three siblings, as well as my large extended family of 49 first cousins and 18 aunts and uncles, often attending multi-generational social events and spending weekends at Lake Superior. I spent most of my time with my family, even though growing up in such a large group of close-knit people felt like a double-edged sword. I always felt loved and supported, but I also felt restricted by their collective traditional outlook. For example, I used to get into trouble for sitting in a corner with a book during family events and special occasions. But that's who I was – I was the geeky, bespectacled, shy, skinny girl who, outside of her own family, struggled to socialize.

In school, I gravitated toward smaller groups of kids when I could find them, and was often more comfortable in the company of boys than girls. Boys seemed more straightforward and transparent, whereas I could never figure out what girls were really up to; boys were friendly to me while girls were mean; and when boys invited me over to their house to play Risk or to listen to a new album, they were there when I arrived and that's what we did. When girls invited me over, they were cruel and unpredictable, if they were even there at all.

Girls' mind games made me feel ugly, stupid and excluded, but with boys, I could build things and play strategic games without feeling that way. So, throughout my childhood and into high school, I found a group of male friends with whom I shared many interests and am still friends with today.

I also spent a lot of time alone growing up, in my head and in books that provided me with the space to dream and imagine. I was involved in a lot of activities, including swimming, tennis, skiing, sailing, piano lessons, dance and choir, but most of all, I loved to read. The library was a weekly destination of mine and, in school, I would read Arthur C. Clarke and Frank Herbert paperbacks under cover of my math textbook. I even enjoyed reading the encyclopedia.

When I wasn't reading, I would lose myself in the active night sky, especially while laying on my back on the dock in the summertime. I wanted to become an astronaut and voyage to the stars, despite the fact that I got car sick and hated roller coasters.

I figured with the way things were going in the late 1960s and early 1970s, that by the time I grew up we would have perfected warp drive and interstellar travel.

That dream ended when I fell into a coma and was diagnosed with Type 1 diabetes at the age of 14. In 1973, when I was given 20 or so years to live a limited life, there were no doctors in our town who knew much about the autoimmune disease. So, my mother became my chief medical expert.

When I fell into the coma, I lost consciousness for an entire day and effectively ceased to exist. I was faced with the reality of my own mortality in two very stark ways: one, I could simply cease to exist without warning, and two, my life expectancy was now very short. Since there was no guarantee I would be alive the next day, I made the decision then that my life had to matter. I knew I wanted to experience as much as I could, and my mother agreed. She said, "This has happened to you. This is your life now. All that matters is how you deal with it. There is no feeling sorry for yourself, no self-indulgence. This is your responsibility and you simply need to accept it."

I decided not long after that I needed to leave my small hometown and get out into the world – and I needed to be able to support myself if I was going to be able to do and see all the things I intended to. So, at 19 years old, I attended the University of Toronto to earn my degree in international relations; a cross-disciplinary study of history, economics and political science. I thought I might be a diplomat. It sounded exciting, all that travel and intrigue, but I also still loved the idea of trying to understand what happened in the world on a global scale and why.

I did well in school, but when I wasn't offered a role in government immediately after graduation, I decided to go to York University Law School. I had thought about becoming a lawyer for some time, but back home, I faced a lot of opposition. In the 1970s and 1980s in Canada, many people still thought being a lawyer was an inappropriate career for a young woman. However, I no longer cared what other people thought I should or shouldn't do with my life – I was following my plan to make my life matter and law seemed like a good match.

In law school, I was interested in how law evolves in the places where creativity and technological advances outpaced the current legal and social infrastructure and pushes up against the thresholds of culture. I thought about becoming an international lawyer, but I was also very interested in intellectual property law.

I learned that there are many aspects of the practice of law that they do not teach you in law school, such as office and gender politics. While articling, men had a huge advantage. The people making the decisions about who got to work on which files were men, and so were their clients. They were not used to women being in law firms other than as secretaries and paralegals, so in general, we were treated as though we had less education and skill than our male colleagues. I started to think that maybe this wasn't the right career for me after all.

After passing my bar exams, I was given an opportunity to clerk for a year in what was then the Supreme Court of Ontario. I was assigned to a panel of four judges to do research, read all of the briefs submitted by counsel, and take notes in court so we could discuss them afterwards and prepare draft judgments for their review.

Even though not all of the judges agreed that women should be lawyers, by the end of the year, I was on great terms with all of them. I was grateful for what they had taught me and felt I had earned their respect. One of the male judges told me I had an "amazing ability to cut through noise and get to the heart of an issue." (Years later, on a decision that had been appealed, he also said, "The Supreme Court of Canada agrees with you and disagrees with me. I'm only going to say this once: you were right.")

Clerking made me want to be a lawyer again. People aren't perfect, and judges are simply that – people with an enormous responsibility over other people's lives. The truth is - most of them take that very seriously and try very hard to get it right. I then decided to become a junior lawyer at a big Bay Street law firm, where I learned a lot about practicing law and approaching and working through complex problems.

Looking up the ladder, though, I couldn't see myself at the top. There were very few senior women and even fewer who were approachable or helpful. Two female partners in particular told me I was "too soft and feminine to make it in this profession" and that I would "eventually need to find a nanny for both day and night so that I could concentrate on my career" – that I just needed to "come home and put money on the table while someone else raised my kids."

I didn't want to be like them, so I went back to York University to obtain my master's degree in law, focusing on the unstated and unacknowledged beliefs that influence decision-makers and how judicial decisions are made. While earning my advanced degree, I worked as a research coordinator for a constitutional law project at the Institute for Public Law and Policy. I love the world of ideas, researching, analyzing and drawing conclusions, but if my work wasn't to have actual life-changing impact or the ability to help people solve their problems, then I didn't feel like what I was doing was enough. I love academia, but it always has to lead back to action in the real world.

Once the report was finished, I went back to my legal practice with a smaller, more specialized firm before becoming a junior lawyer in a mid-sized firm. Most of the time, my male colleagues were nothing but complimentary, telling me I had "a way of finding a deal and leading parties to it" and that I was "great at building teams, systems, businesses, relationships and solutions." I also found that the combination of intellectual property, international relations and business knowledge gave me a very powerful skill set to approach issues facing many companies.

The world was beginning to realize the value of intellectual property assets as drivers of wealth and innovation.

I was still not a fan of the gender discrimination and sexual harassment that came with working in a firm. My next step was to co-found my own experimental boutique firm to have control over my practice and to be able to choose which clients I wanted to work with. That so many clients followed me to my new, unproven firm was very satisfying, and within our firm, a modular "practice-in-association" model worked best. "Eat what you kill" may not work for everyone, but we were happy with the fact that while we shared general expenses, our practices were financially separate.

I next took a professional risk in becoming Vice President and General Counsel for a small pharmaceutical company, because having just one client doesn't mean less work. It means you are on duty 24/7, especially when it comes to international business. I also took personal risks with high-risk pregnancies and miscarriages throughout my career until I gave birth to two healthy sons, for whom I subsequently took time out of my career. I successfully resisted the message I got at the time from the profession, which was, "You will never work again at a high level."

Today, I am an international legal and business consultant on intellectual property strategy and commercial transactions. Though I now value independence more than I value money, prestige or recognition, I still love solving puzzles, bringing innovative new technologies to market and working with innovative business leaders to achieve their goals around the world.

As a woman leader, I was often underestimated, undermined and excluded from both business deals and social events, but I had the determination, courage and confidence to do things on my own terms without changing my essential nature to be like anyone else or meet anyone else's idea of who I should be. I challenged myself to take risks and join organizations, serve on committees, give seminars and workshops, and go to conferences year after year until I was known, trusted and included.

If you work for me, I expect you to give your very best, too, and to continuously strive to improve. I am supportive but certainly not a micro-manager. I like people to try to solve problems themselves and come to me with suggested solutions when they have taken things as far as they can. I like to unleash potential in people by helping them believe in themselves and their ability to learn and handle new challenges. I am interested in developing the next generation of leaders, so I push people to exceed their own expectations of themselves.

Others might think I am tough to work for because my standards are very high, but I apply the same standards to others as I apply to myself: work hard, be smart and take your job seriously. If you are clear about what is important to you and the priorities that you want to achieve, I strongly believe that you can plan and execute accordingly.

Women still face issues in the workplace that men do not. While the barriers to entry for many traditional male careers are much lower than they were when I first started, the fine balance between career and family is still far more difficult for women to navigate than for men, as the expectation is still that a woman will make herself available for child and elder care no matter what her career responsibilities might be. Then there is the common catch-22 that a woman will be criticized for putting family ahead of work but also for putting her career ahead of family.

I think we need to find ways of supporting women so that they can offload some of this mental burden. For instance, I never liked the idea of having to do all my work at the office. I found that I could be just as productive, or even more so, if I could work remotely part of the time. This allowed me to attend to family responsibilities, which often times were time-rigid and out of my control, and also complete work responsibilities.

Regardless, women leaders still need to be able to clearly define their priorities in ways that men often do not. A woman, for example, must establish herself as a credible and dominant leader without also appearing tyrannical or inflexible. She must somehow strike a balance between being emotionally available and likable but also must be cool-headed in a crisis. At the end of the day, a man is still judged more on the results of his leadership than his leadership style while a woman is judged on both, as well as her physical appearance.

I have five key pieces of advice by which to navigate one's career in this type of high-powered environment:

1. Learn to think like the person on the other side of the conversation and you will be a better communicator and negotiator.

2. Look beyond what is being said and done on the public stage to better understand the context, importance and impact of events.
3. Be careful who you go into business with – due diligence with prospective partners, colleagues and clients is critical – and don't believe any promises. Always get it in writing.
4. You don't need to say "yes" to every request for your time and input. If you say "no" sometimes, it will be okay. I, too, tend to oversubscribe myself, because I can usually see what needs to be done and how to do it. But you don't owe anyone anything!
5. You can't control what other people think, and a confident, successful woman is always going to be the subject of speculation and rumors. Just keep your head up, be true to yourself, and keep showing them how good you are at what you do. Over and over again.

If nothing else, remember this: a good leader has vision, intelligence, drive and ambition; she knows how to inspire people and help people achieve their best; when to push forward in spite of resistance and when to change course; and she is capable of making decisions with the information available to her at the time and not waiting until things are perfect, as things will never be perfect.

We can and must, however, continue to strive for balance. This means that all aspects of our selves are valued, cared for and allocated adequate time and resources to thrive. Physical, emotional, professional, artistic and intellectual health are all given equal importance in my life, though I have rarely, if ever, achieved equilibrium, since these shift constantly. One thing I am absolutely committed to, however, is proper diet, sleep and exercise – if I don't take care of these things, nothing else is possible.

My alarm clock goes off these days at 7:15 a.m. and if I don't get out of bed, my dog comes and gets me so we can take our daily one-hour morning walk through the woods behind our house in Toronto, where I live with my husband. I then like to deal with complex problems without interruption. Though I read email throughout the day, I've disabled notifications so that I am not interrupted. I also try to schedule calls and meetings for after 11:00 a.m. when I am most productive.

In the afternoon, I follow up on administrative tasks and emails before taking my dog for another hour-long walk around

6:oo p.m. Dinner is typically around 7:00 p.m. and often I'm back to work in the evening to tie up loose ends and plan for the next day.

Prior to going to sleep at 11:00 p.m., I unwind with music, a book or a television show, unless I'm out listening to live music, attending a play or having dinner with friends, then it can be quite late.

I also try not to work on the weekends, but rather devote my time to personal interests and my social life, as well as fitness, sleep and health. I run errands and try to get organized for the next week by planning meals and resupplying our household. I also like to paint, sing jazz, write creatively, ski, hike, and volunteer in both the arts and healthcare. And, my husband and I like to cook on the weekends, when we actually have time to spend in the kitchen.

I also go to the barn and visit with my horse, sometimes saddling him up to go for a ride. I decided at forty years old that I wanted to learn how to ride horses and I did so, despite the risks and dangers of the sport. I am proud that I never gave up on myself and that, despite my supposed limitations, I pushed through many barriers to achieve the life and career I wanted.

POUND ON!!

My idea of success has evolved over the years. It used to mean being the successful lawyer making tons of money and gaining professional recognition. Now, while those things are still important, they are no longer sufficient. Now, success is more about being at peace with myself and with who I am and being able to choose how I spend my time without worrying about what other people think. Now is the time for me.

Pictured: Vacations are critical to recharge for the challenges we face. Lynda with her husband, Jim Fabro.

Pictured: Listening is just as important as singing. Music is a collaboration.

Pictured: In balance with one of my greatest teachers.

POUND ON!!

SALLY GLICK

The best and most generous networker you'll ever meet, Sally Glick is a partner in a successful accounting firm. While not even an accountant herself, her remarkable talent at marketing and forging client connections has made her an indispensable asset to the firm.

Sally started her career in her father's accounting firm, learning marketing through experience and tenacity, and later earning an MBA. A passionate mentor and educator, Sally raised 3 children as a single parent while building her impressive career. A loving grandmother, Sally's selfless devotion to family and friends is unequaled, and appreciated by all.

POUND ON!!

SALLY GLICK

The Consummate Marketer and Mentor

Those who know me well know my work has had a very positive impact on my life, connecting me with amazing women and men whom I never would have known if not for my career trajectory. But what people don't always recognize is that building meaningful relationships by being a connector and helping others is the most fun work one could ever dream of.

As a leader who leads by example, I rarely ask others to do something I cannot or have not done. I do my best to explain the big picture to our team so that they know exactly why they are performing key tasks and how their results impact the firm. I assume responsibility, take ownership and bring energy and passion to the table to help achieve exciting results. Mostly I think

I am Alpha material because I choose to pave the way for others, especially women. While men have plenty of great mentors and opportunities for advancement, I believe it is women who need more.

Having begun my career working with my father, a career which lasted more than 20 years, I do not believe I faced as many traditional challenges as other women had. My father helped carve a path to success for me without ever treating me as if I were simply a "kid." Instead, from the beginning, he demonstrated how strongly he respected my abilities and my commitment to my work, giving me the latitude and credibility expected for a more seasoned professional. In return, I did everything I could to deserve his confidence, a lesson I carried with me from my childhood years.

I grew up in an incredibly warm and culturally diverse environment on the famous South Side of Chicago. As was common in the 1950s, most of my extended family, from my cousins to my great-great-grandfather, all lived nearby and I had the privilege of knowing them throughout my childhood. This included my adoring maternal grandmother, who was a very strong influence on me. When my grandfather died suddenly in his early

50s, my grandmother, having never worked outside the home, rose to the challenge to make my grandfather's dry-cleaning business more profitable than ever. It turned out that my grandmother, who resembled a beautiful Loretta Young, had a mind for business and loved people. I thought she was fearless and I loved spending time with her. My grandmother learned to love traveling and vacationing alone, especially to winter in warmer climates, and she was very adventurous without once needing to ever enter another relationship. She used to say she married once for love but never again wanted to find some "old man's slippers under her bed," which was very independent thinking for a woman who would be 111 years old today.

My mother, on the other hand, drove infrequently and did not like to venture too far outside of her own neighborhood. She was not much of a risk taker given that my father would take care of whatever she needed, so she would not often have to leave her comfort zone. My mother had finished high school and then followed my father in the Navy awhile before taking on the responsibilities of home and childcare at the age of twenty-two.

My father finished school, passed the bar and become a practicing attorney before realizing he hated it for being too unethical. When he returned to school, he discovered he loved accounting and therefore became a solo certified public accountant with a growing practice, despite never having a staff of more than seven. I learned later in life that in my early years, this resulted in not much time or money for dining out or vacations, but I always felt my life was luxuriously happy.

My mother's fear, however, would only intensify the year I turned 11. My sister, three years younger than I, often would play make-believe games like "house" and "school" with me as we shared a bedroom. But when I was ten years old, my sister died of childhood Leukemia at the age of 8. It changed everything for me, in that I went from having a sister to being a lonely only child – and it also certainly changed my parents. Though they grew stronger as a couple, united in their commitment to raise me to be as normal and independent as possible, I knew then that I shouldered a special responsibility as their only remaining child to refrain from misbehaving in any significant way. After all, my mother's greatest desire was to keep me safe, which sometimes prevented me from doing the things I wanted. For example, she did not like me going near swimming pools or roller skating rinks, and I remained good about toeing the line all while attending Chicago public high school. I still had a wide circle of wonderful friends, most of whom I remain in close contact with today. My friendships helped me maintain a strong, moral attitude as a down-to-earth South Sider, reinforcing the lessons I had learned throughout my life so that I would continue to be a good person and help others.

I would go on to work with my father every summer in high school at his firm before attending Washington University in 1967 to study speech therapy. I then transferred to Northwestern University in 1968 and took on psychology as a minor, as I loved the concept of understanding how people make choices. When I married in 1969, however, I left school to work with my father full-time. I needed a job to help continue to put my now ex-husband through school, and my dad needed help in the office identifying new business opportunities. He said he was looking for a marketing director who could work and speak with people, be articulate and figure out a way to set up seminars, partnerships and events. Looking back, I am dumbfounded that he trusted me to take on this critical role, but I accepted the challenge and together we ultimately grew his firm to nearly $1 million. At the time, this was a huge accomplishment and represented great success.

The plan had been for me to go back to school and eventually move on, but it was such an amazing experience that it impacted my entire life. My father recognized skills in me that I didn't even know I had, and I realize now that it was my father who pushed me to become the kind of professional I am today.
He simply assumed I could do the jobs he gave me and reassured me that I didn't have to be an accountant to be his marketing director – I just needed to understand how to make money and deal with people.

Still, it was certainly trial by fire to start. There were never any classes to learn how to best accomplish professional services marketing. I simply learned from my father how to be energetic, passionate and committed in my career, as he loved connecting with and promoting other people as much as he did being a great dad and husband. I saw then how hard my father worked to bring in business and what a good provider he was, so I never once felt burdened by all the responsibility he entrusted in me. I frequently went out into the community, attending events, talking to bankers and attorneys, joining chambers of commerce and giving seminars. I also completed small business tasks like bank reconciliations, sales tax returns, payroll processing and basic bookkeeping on top of branding and business development. I even had to learn to work a giant bookkeeping machine as there were no automated programs like there are today. As frustrating as it was for me, it was phenomenal to watch my dad in his element. I would be working on a bank reconciliation for thirty minutes, to the point that you could see all the eraser marks, and I'd say, "Dad, I'm still off by $1.50." And he'd say, "It's in there somewhere. You cannot turn this bank reconciliation around until this is the same number as this." Then he'd peer over my shoulder and say, "Check this number." I'd check again and it was almost always a transposition error or a missing service charge – one he could easily find in a heartbeat.

I believed my dad to be the smartest person I would ever meet. While we interacted at the office every day, it was our out-of-office conversations over dinner or at family events where I truly benefited from his wisdom and amazing leadership skills. More than once, my mother unsuccessfully tried to enforce a rule prohibiting us from "talking business" at dinner, but my dad and I just couldn't help ourselves.

It is no surprise, then, that the most interesting facet of marketing to me was getting involved in the community, spending time cultivating future clients and nurturing existing relationships to promote high retention and loyalty – just like my father. I realize now how critical self-awareness is when it comes to emotional intelligence in the workplace, but in my earlier years I was more focused on my technical skills and competencies. Now, however, I believe these are second to those soft skills that will help lead others to success in the workplace.

My dad taught me to always look at things through different lenses and perspectives. For example, when I first meet someone at an event today, I try to think about how I can help them, even if there's no immediate need or reward. Should I reach out to them? How can I get to know them better? Is there an opportunity for them to shine? Why not nominate them for an award? Maybe there will be a work benefit, maybe not, but if I find things in common with someone, I try to connect. This may not be traditional marketing, but it works. It creates relationships that are long-lasting and even friendships when you are not expecting them. I've been told that this kind of activity is selfless, generous and uncommon. But frankly, I enjoy seeing others succeed and I know it means a lot to other people because we don't always stop to help or recognize others enough.

My father taught me that we need to treat clients differently than anyone else in order to gain their trust and grow business. "Wear your psychiatrist hat," he would tell me, and "find out what the most important thing is to the client to create a special bond." Working with him was like going to a mini-MBA program every day, and I am very grateful for what I learned from him.

I only left my father's firm in 1973 to have my first child; my second in 1975; and my last in 1978. I learned from motherhood the patience it requires to put someone ahead of yourself, though I loved them with a fierceness I never knew I had. It was and still is the kind of love that had me exhaustingly typing papers for them at 10pm while doing laundry after coming home from a traveling baseball tournament so my son would have a clean uniform for his next game.

Mothers tend to be nurturers, and I was no exception. But sometimes, this stops us from pursuing all of our career goals at various times. Today, for example, I don't see many women at 7:00 a.m. meetings, as they are getting their kids off to school while their husbands network over breakfast. That is why I still believe we need women-specific events - I'd rather see us together than separate, but we are not there yet. At least now we are aware. We know what is going on and we are no longer invisible. We can be more successful if we fight for ourselves and are courageous, even though the responsibilities of raising children may still provide obstacles. I am hopeful for change.

When I left the workforce for motherhood, my father found a replacement to continue basic bookkeeping for the firm. However, the woman he hired simply could not keep up. In fact, the day after I had my first baby my father arrived at the hospital with a bag full of invoices, asking if I would place them in alphabetical order for the accounting system. I did, to the horror and amazement of my hospital roommate, but I did not think anything of it. I was 25 years old and had just had my first baby, but I knew my dad needed my help.

Working for a family business has both its benefits and its downsides. You have a sense of pride and ownership, but with that comes great responsibility. You also have very little independence because you can never truly get away from your family. They control you with money even though you have security. I know other women did not have the kind of support I had, but even that can bind you in ways that can be exhausting.

My mother did offer to babysit while I spent one evening a week organizing my father's office. However, her fear for me returned when I got divorced at the age of 31. She believed my marriage would help keep me safe, but instead, I would now be alone. For me, however, this was my evolution from being a young adult into a real one. I had never lived on my own and this probably was the only way I ever would. I needed a job that would allow me to create a workday around my kids' schedules. So, I returned to work full-time with my father's firm in 1980.

I would leave for work once the kids boarded the school bus and I would leave the downtown area at 3:30 p.m. so I was home by 4:00 p.m. each day to greet them. I don't know when the phrase "flexible work hours" came into the lexicon but it wasn't ever that it wasn't an issue or that it wasn't addressed – it simply was that no one ever said, "I want to come to work and be flexible." You went to work and that was your only thought. When I went back to work with my father, it was very convenient and safe. I was never going to lose my job. If I needed my check early, I could get it. I never had to act like a single parent with three kids, juggling work and home, because for better or for worse, they were one.

I am still pretty autonomous in my career today, but nothing beats working for my father and the partnership and trust we shared. My dad knew what I was capable of, what I was accomplishing and my commitment. If I worked remotely or was out of the office, he knew I was being productive. Too often I speak with business owners or partners at professional services firms who believe out of sight means loafing, but great leaders choose their staff wisely knowing trust is imperative. In fact, I did most of my networking while at Little League games, being the class mom, carpooling and organizing school fairs. As the neighborhood changed and other mothers did not know what was required or needed for activities, I took on the task of teaching them so that they and their children would have good experiences, too. I never thought it was hard; I thought it was fun. We had to go above and beyond in our own community, you see, as a small firm who often could not compete. For example, I often would make it a priority to stop in at Palatine, Illinois on my way home to Buffalo Grove. Why? Midas Mufflers.

My dad had a client who owned one Midas Mufflers franchise and ultimately ended up owning four, but he never outgrew our firm. When he told us that all of their franchisees were trained in Palatine, I made it a point to meet with their office manager. I explained that my father had done a great job of training his client on how to run a business – things like how to open bank accounts, how to negotiate better interest rates with credit cards and how to successfully read financial statements. I told her our firm would be willing to continue that sort of training for all of their franchisees for free. The office manager said she would think about it and the put the proposal in a drawer.

I kept returning for well over two years with Bulls tickets and other incentives to keep us at the top of their mind. When that office manager retired and a new person came in, I got a phone call. I said this would give us a chance to share business information that everyone would be smarter for. The new office manager agreed but thought it would be more appropriate to bring in Merrill Lynch. I told her I understood the size and prestige of Merrill Lynch, but asked if she would give us a try also with a couple of training sessions over the next few months. That resulted in an easy win. My dad was passionate about this work whereas Merrill Lynch's employees were simply there to do a job. From the ground up, my father, with his experience as a sole practitioner, walked those franchisees through everything they needed for about ten years. He also was exposed to business owners across the country, some of whom changed their accounting over to our firm over time.

With our nonprofit group at SobelCo, the objective is the same – to be immersed in the community, to know all the key players, to provide training and to always be in front of the decision makers. That's what my father and I did in 1982, and it continues to work today, no matter how big or small your company is.

It takes a lot of hard work, but if one is able to prioritize what matters most and create one's own sense of balance, women, too, can manage to have it all. Holding fast to one's core values and focusing on what is most important, women can engage in targeted pursuits of what is most critical for them and their ambitions. For me, sometimes that meant asking the exterminator who came twice a year to stay with my youngest son while I ran the older two kids to the early bus for band practice. Sometimes that meant asking my mother to come to work with us when my son had strep throat for the thousandth time. We would take my son, bundled up in his pajamas, to my father's office in the high rise we worked at in Chicago. My mother would sit with him on the couch, read and color with him, feed him soup and watch him while he napped before we all got in the car and went home.

I never missed a minute of work because those things can happen when you work with family, but other women often have the additional stress of such responsibilities to juggle along with their career. When their male partners are encouraged to accept more personal responsibilities and the salaries for women increase, the situation will equalize. I believe future generations are moving swiftly toward this much more equitable approach. In fact, when my eldest son's wife declared that being a mom was difficult, my son made a gratifying comment that he didn't know how I had done it all by myself. I don't know either. I just knew I didn't have a choice.

I loved being a mother and raising my children. I'd like to think my children learned to be contributing, content and kind people from me.

In 1994, with my mother's health declining before she passed from Alzheimer's in her late 60s, my father merged his practice with a larger firm of 40 people, in contrast with our five. They had never heard of a marketing director but my job with my dad was always to form great relationships, so I continued to become friendly with their clients. One in particular was a manufacturer of fasteners who I often would clip industry articles for and have her son spend time with mine. However, one day one of the partners complained to me that if his client had a question, she would call me first. They were offended at how deeply my relationships went but it was the only way I knew how. That is what my dad taught me.

I moved on to Pencor Mazur, a company that provided marketing tools for accounting firms nationwide. Yet, even though I stopped working for my father, I would do marketing webinars that he would surreptitiously watch. He would even ask questions to make sure I knew he was there. I also returned to school and finally graduated in 1998 before earning an executive MBA from Lake Forest Graduate School of Business Management in 2000. I never even viewed my job as a career until then, when I realized employees from other companies were attending the program at their company's expense. I was paying my own way, which made me feel different. I also felt like a stranger to the business learnings when I didn't even speak the same language. What was a KPI? A benchmark? EBITDA? My dad had never educated me in such things. I only did marketing and administrative work, even though I also was growing the business and marketing our brand.

I later moved to Atlanta, Georgia to work with an international accounting association, Alluvial Global, before one of its member firms, Videre Group, hired and relocated me to New Jersey in 2002. I met Alan Sobel at a local event and got to know him, so when my firm merged with J.H. Cohn in 2005, I left for SobelCo.

My father, my greatest mentor, passed at the age of 80. But I learned how to develop the power of connections from him while understanding that it is more important to give than to get. That philosophy is still at the core of everything I do here. I love my role at SobelCo as the firm's ambassador. It is my joy to represent the firm in the business and nonprofit communities and to interact with business owners and nonprofit leaders, nurturing and cultivating sustainable relationships. My day includes a mix of traditional marketing activities, such as crafting proposals and presentations, scheduling events, researching and writing articles for our firm's website, newsletter and social media, and guiding and mentoring our professionals in their own marketing initiatives. It's nice to be able to add value, especially when someone is in transition or trying to figure out their next journey. What also really matters to me is the faith and willingness my firm had to name me as their first woman partner, keeping in mind that I am not a certified public accountant. That was quite a leap of faith, and the impact of that message resonates with me every day.

Everyone should be advanced based on their competency and capabilities. Even if a woman cannot take on the most complex case load involving weeks of travel, if she is bright, articulate, and an excellent employee, she should advance even if she isn't commuting to California weekly. Today, I would tell women to be kind and bold. I would tell them to ask for what they think is fair. I would have them set goals for themselves so they can track their own success and celebrate their progress. I would tell them not to get discouraged but instead to take 100 percent control over their own careers. I would urge them to be smart, passionate and exude energy and confidence.

Still, as great as it would be to point to the many accomplishments and milestones of women in the workplace, change is so slow that it is difficult to remain positive. In the current professional climate, women still need to work harder to demonstrate greater competencies. They need to focus on being strong without being aggressive; flexible without seeming weak; seeking feedback without seeming unsure; relevant without being too serious. In short, they still need to be more careful regarding the ramifications of their behavior.

In my experience, women tend to lead better when building camaraderie and consensus. Men are traditionally seen as more authoritative leaders but given the attitudes of collaborative millennials who like to work on teams, it would seem the leadership style more commonly adopted by women will be much more successful in the decades ahead.

I'm risk averse but I raised children who are not afraid of a thing, with my son currently living in Bangkok after relocating his family to Guam, my worldly daughter recently moving from Boston to Chicago, and my other son currently taking two years away from his work in Chicago to live with his family in Turin, Italy. It's pretty cool that they were never held back by their mother. I love that adventurous spirit about them.

With my three adult children now living around the world, the people I spend the most time with include a wide range of business professionals and friends in New Jersey whom I have met over the years after networking unfettered. I am the luckiest person I know given who my friends are and how much fun we have together, as well as how much we support each other at all times. I am involved and engaged in so many different events, programs and groups that I just cannot get home as early or consistently as my two cats and my new rescue dog Rocco would like.

I also like to read great books and try different wines to relax. I visit with friends, see movies, run errands and devote a few hours each weekend to writing for the firm. Still, best of all is traveling to visit and vacation with my family. I do often get on planes alone and brave overnight stays at airport hotels to go and visit them. How else would I get to see them? I simply have to figure it out.

For me, success is a life well-lived with family and friends while keeping in perspective what truly matters most. I would not say that I have ever truly worked toward a professional legacy of my own, but I have always been committed to helping others achieve theirs, especially if I have the connections and resources to help them accomplish their goals. I would rather have a reputation for being nice and leveraging my own career to help others than anything else.

When a colleague tells me that I have had a positive impact on his or her life, professionally or personally, that is the best compliment and endorsement for me and my efforts. It validates my goals as a woman in business helping others and I truly could not be happier.

Pictured: Sally, her son, her granddaughter and her Father at her NJBIZ top 50 women award in 2009.

Pictured: Sally's Father, Harold Leftwich.

Pictured: Sally with two of her children and her Father at the Northern New Jersey Visiting Nurses Gala, where she was an honoree.

CHERYL GOLDHART

An internationally renowned and award-winning Family Law Lawyer, Cheryl is a true Alpha entrepreneur. A law school graduate at the top of her class, Cheryl went on to work in a big Bay Street law firm before founding her own firm.

Cheryl's generosity to family and friends is beyond measure, both in terms of skill, time, love and advice. As a teacher and mentor she gives back to the profession and is highly respected for her negotiation, mediation, and arbitration skills. The first of her family to go to University, Cheryl earned a B.A. from York University, an L.L.B. from the University of Western Ontario and an M.A. in counseling from University of Toronto (O.I.S.E).

POUND ON!!

CHERYL GOLDHART

From Comedy Shop to Courtroom

Having practiced family law for more than thirty years, I can tell you that it's sort of like being a nun – you either have a calling to do this work, or you shouldn't be doing it at all. It also brings with it a better understanding of yourself and the family you grew up with.

My parents met in Toronto when they were teenagers, after my grandparents emigrated from eastern Europe to Canada at the turn of the century.

My father's father, from what I can remember, was the kind of guy who would figure out how much money he needed that day and would quit working if he had earned it by 10 a.m. He lived a long, stress-free life. My father worked for a hardworking uncle who had built a large international auto parts company, and his work ethic was much different. After leading a highly successful division of the business for many years, he ultimately inherited the company in the 1980s when his uncle died and continued running it until he retired, and it was sold.

My mother, though born into a more financially secure family than my father, also ran her own business. As she did not enjoy being an isolated housewife, raising a family in a rather undeveloped area of Toronto, she started a jewelry and antique business out of the home, despite lacking any business training.

Soon, loyal customers would repeatedly visit her for her advice on all things bejeweled and beautiful, as she grew to become a fabulous marketer of shiny vintage items. So, at a time when few mothers worked, my entrepreneurial mother built and sustained a thriving, well-known retail business, which she quickly relocated to a retail store in an upscale Toronto neighborhood.

This is the kind of success I would look up to and the work ethic I was encouraged to achieve. Education would never be a priority in our home, as neither of my parents attended college, but working hard to make money was.

Still, childhood came first. I remember visiting our family's cottage each summer , with my mother, sister and I staying for days at a time while my father and the other men joined us on Friday evenings for big family dinners. I also remember my sister and I spending a lot of weekends with my aunt, who was a therapist, my blind uncle and our older cousins, which offered quite a different experience than my own nuclear family had.

I also had a lot of friends in school and in the neighborhood, but never of the popular kind. I attended all sorts of lessons from ballet to piano, but I wasn't very good at anything, much to the dismay of my talented mother.

Then, when I was a teenager, I found standup comedy. A place called Yuk Yuks had started up in the basement of a church and I used to go with friends to open mic nights, in which comedians such as Jim Carrey and Howie Mandel would perform. I also spent a lot of time trying it myself, which was interesting and fun. But my father, being completely unimpressed with my comedic ambitions, repeatedly discouraged me by telling me how little comedians earned and that I would never make any money.

This was not exactly the best thing for a lazy, misdirected, floundering soul to hear, especially when I wasn't the greatest or the most motivated of students. So, naturally, I dropped out of high school during grade twelve. There was quite an argument with my parents about my decision, but ultimately, I went to work in my mother's shop.

For nearly a year I would work during the day and perform stand-up comedy at night. Then, one day a wealthy regular came in to browse, speak with my mother, and perhaps purchase a bauble. I distinctly remember her Persian lamb suit with mink fur accents and the beautiful brand-new Rolls Royce she had parked outside. When I asked her if I could take a look at her car, she said, "Sure, honey, and while you're at it, you can wash it for me, too!"

I nearly collapsed under the weight of that insult. Determined never to allow anyone to treat me like that again, I decided to go back to school and learn something so that I would never again be in such a position.

I attended night school and summer school to catch back up and chose my courses more carefully so that I would be more interested in the subject matter. For example, I developed a particular interest in sociology and psychology because people who go into psychotherapy typically have issues themselves that they need to work out. I thought maybe I could help people help themselves (even though I learned later in life that most people cannot).

I worked so hard that I got a scholarship to earn my Bachelor of Arts in the subject from York University in 1982. However, I earned my undergraduate degree while living at home, and I eventually felt the need to leave to make something of myself. So, I applied to Western University Law, two hours from Toronto.

I knew no one who was a lawyer. I didn't even really know what a lawyer did, exactly. The most I ever learned about the law was from my cousin, whose exploits regularly required the services of a criminal lawyer. So, I never in a million years dreamed that I would be accepted, but I thought, why not try? I was shocked to have received an acceptance letter. I thought someone had made a huge mistake in letting me in. Were they really going to let me be a lawyer? I apparently was not the only one who felt this way. One of the first things I heard in law school was a male student telling me that I had taken away a spot at the university from another man.

And, to make matters worse, everything about the coursework was indeed completely foreign to me.

In law school, you are always under some kind of deadline or pressure, because that is what the actual workload is like. That is why the Law School Admission Test has a time limit, so that you are forced to get the questions right while struggling to keep up. The skillset requires being able to absorb tons of information within a short amount of time to then apply it to a problem.

Needless to say, my first year of law school was extremely stressful. However, I soon met my husband, Harvey, who helped teach me how to study properly – and I met Professor Jay McLeod. Widely known as the brilliant family law expert of my generation, Jay was a rather unkempt, polarizing kind of instructor, but given my interest in psychology and sociology (let alone the complexities of my own family dynamics), I always found his courses appealing and fascinating. I found him to be funny while others found him to be difficult, and I happened to do well in his classes. So, I of course took every class he offered.

After making it through my first year, the second year was better, and, quite to my own complete shock, I truly excelled in my third. I was stunned out of mind that I could do this, but graduate I did with a Bachelor of Laws in 1985. I was no longer that high school dropout – I was going to be a lawyer and I was actually going to make a living.

Articling nearly killed that dream. I completed my required 10-month apprenticeship at a large downtown firm in Toronto, but it was a fate worse than death. Yes, it was highly competitive; yes, we worked extremely long hours with little respect; and, of course the work was boring. But mostly, I didn't like the people I had to work with. You see, my father was in the middle of selling his company at the time, and my law firm coincidentally would be representing the sale. Everyone therefore knew my business and either dealt with me with "kid gloves" or would treat me poorly because they assumed I got the job solely because my father was a huge client. Every day grew increasingly uncomfortable. Then, to make matters worse, Harvey called off our engagement three weeks before our impending wedding (but more on this later).

I was so demoralized by the entire experience that I decided to return to my previous interest in psychology and go back to school to earn my master's degree in counseling, which I would ultimately earn from the University of Toronto in 1986. I thought I would become a mediator, and so, when I ran into Jay at a conference, I asked for his advice. Could I start a mediation practice for family law? Was there work? Could I make a living?

Jay didn't think there was enough business, and the gentleman he was sitting with, Stephen Grant, told me that I couldn't be a good mediator without having practiced family law. Having also been my bar admission course instructor, Stephen and I chatted further as we boarded an escalator at the conference. Then, he offered me a job. I didn't even really know who he was, but his large downtown firm was looking to hire, and I said, okay! I worked at Gowlings, Strathy and Hendersen (later Gowlings) for seventeen years, working my way up to partner under the mentorship of Stephen, who was one of the major players in the area at the time.

Stephen was the first to teach me to start crafting a good reputation from day one because that is all you have. Being a good and respectable lawyer means not always taking your clients' positions just because that is what your client says to do. I mostly learned by osmosis while watching Stephen in a courtroom.

I had an immediate credibility with judges and other lawyers simply by being associated with Stephen and was therefore able to interact with the most senior members of the bar. I also was protected – no one started up with me because they knew they would have to deal with him. He was a rainmaker at the firm, and I was under his umbrella.

But while Stephen taught me to be a barrister, it was Karon Bales who taught me the skills of a solicitor. Karon, a daughter of a well-known politician in Toronto, took over his law practice and gracefully handled whatever it was that came across her desk with a stiff upper lip. When she gave birth to her children, she returned from maternity leave within two days, despite not believing it was right. She was a woman who certainly worked to earn the credibility she deserved.

You see, women in law at the time had to be even more organized and direct than normal but still were expected not to rock the boat too much. You had to overcome being a shrinking violet without being rude while also being able to tell people what you want and what you believe is right without appearing inappropriate. It was a delicate balancing act.

Still, I learned everything I needed to learn to be the lawyer I am today from my time at Gowlings, while balancing all of my personal responsibilities in a way that worked best for the most important people in my life.

I gave birth to my twins in 1990 with my first husband, whom I abruptly dated, too quickly married and ultimately divorced after my engagement to Harvey was called off. My youngest, however, was born in 1996 with Harvey, whom I had previously avoided as we had worked in the same building – but that could only last so long. When we saw each other again, we knew, and we took it from where we left off to get married in 1994.

While I now have an extremely good marriage for someone who is a family lawyer, I learned during my time at Gowlings that you simply cannot do it all. Harvey and I, for example, both worked full-time and therefore needed to hire a nanny. That's what worked for us and we were okay with it. You simply cannot be the best mother, the best in your career, and have a great social life – to push yourself to do and have it all is a mistake because something will eventually give. It might be your marriage, or your kids might be messed up, or you won't do well at work, but if you can realize early on how to designate the time and effort that works for you to each of these things, everything can remain balanced. Heck, I even found the time to serve as both the Family Law Executive Chair for the Ontario Bar Association and as a member of the Canadian Bar Association, as well as sitting on numerous other committees during this time. It can be done, and I had figured it out!

But then I started talking to Avra Rosen. Avra and I had been friends in high school (her first husband was actually my first boyfriend), and though we went our separate ways in university, we both ended up working in family law in Toronto. So, Avra and I got back in touch, she had started her own practice and she encouraged me to do the same.

For a long time, though, I was too afraid. I was well supported by a firm, after all, who handled all the accounting, photocopying, word processing and more. These were things I never even had to think about. But still, Avra persisted in her encouragement.

When I expressed an interest in leaving to my partners at Gowlings, they were more than happy to continue supporting me in my journey. After all, family law in a big law firm was not as profitable, and the business model typically wasn't a great fit. So, when I said that I wanted to strike out on my own and start my own firm, they told me to take all of my clients with me. And, because of my work with Stephen, I was able to develop a high net worth clientele.

So, I hit the ground running as president of Goldhart & Associates in 2004, sharing office space with Avra and working with just one associate and two assistants. I even found that the minute I left I made double the money!

Looking back, I was able to strategically use the lucky parts of my life to my advantage. Yes, I was strangely accepted into law school, but I went and did well. Yes, Stephen offered me a job, but I took it and worked hard to make a name for myself. I took every opportunity to build on my luck toward success and have done everything expected of me and more.

Today, I am a practiced litigator, mediator and arbitrator, spending nearly half of my time helping to resolve disputes or make decisions instead of bringing a case to court in front of a judge. My multimillion-dollar family law firm is larger than typical with a staff of fifteen, but many times over, I have encouraged associates to do as I did to become my own lawyer, because why sit second chair their whole lives? I must be an advocate.

I thought, perhaps, that I might become a judge after leaving Gowlings, but judges in Canada report to a boss – the chief justice and Canadian government. And, when I started my own practice, I thought, why didn't I do this years ago? So, although I have been presented with opportunities to pursue this line of work over the last few years, I would now rather spend my "spare" time mentoring and supervising my staff to make them better at what they do. There is far too much value in being your own boss.

However, because of my unlikely financial success as a family lawyer in Toronto, I also make it a point to give back. For example, I currently serve on the Family Law Bench and Bar Committee, which acts as a liaison between judges, the courts and the family law bar in Ontario; the Family Law Arbitration Executive Committee; the Unified Family Court Expansion Group; the Attorney General Committee, which develops protocols for reform regarding complaints against assessors; as Chair of the Dispute Resolution Officer Program, which runs a group of lawyers who conduct conferences at the court to resolve and narrow issues in cases, which conducts education and training; and, most recently was appointed by Canadian Parliament to serve on the Judicial Advisory Committee, which reviews and recommends candidates for judicial appointment.

I really enjoy the committee work because I love to do things that assist the court, other family lawyers, and most importantly, families in Ontario. I also am a frequent guest speaker and instructor in all matters regarding family law, including the issues of mediation, physical and emotional abuse, spousal and child support, power imbalances, wills and estates, custody agreements and more.

All of this has led to me being the only family lawyer in Ontario to be awarded the Lexpert Zenith Award in 2014 and my earning the Ontario Bar Association's Award for Excellence in Family Law in 2016. Named in honor of Jay, earning this prestigious award has been the highlight of my legal career, and I am extremely proud and humbled to have accepted it in front of my children and parents.

When people ask what I do, I like to say that I help people as opposed to saying I am a lawyer. I do my best work when I am able to help people get through difficult situations, using my skills to move them through a very difficult process while getting them what they need and what they are entitled to and causing the least damage to their loved ones as possible.

After all, you do the best you can with the cards you are dealt, and to get through it without being damaged yourself or damaging anyone else is certainly an achievement – one I know all too well.

Harvey retired from his career as a lawyer nearly three years ago and we travel more frequently than we ever had to places such as Europe and Asia. Though we live in Toronto , we often summer at a cottage up north and winter in Florida.

My younger sister, who married her high school sweetheart and settled closer to home, now runs my mother's store. Though we pursued very different dreams, we are now much closer than we used to be.

My youngest daughter, now in her second year of law school at Western University, sometimes comes home on the weekends to visit, and I also try to spend as much time as possible vacationing with my other two children and three grandchildren.

Overall, I am thankful to be in a good place today despite my own past obstacles, and I would say that my life, now, is truly blessed.

LEE INNOCENTI

A true Alpha and entrepreneur, Dr. Lee Innocenti is the Founder and Principal of Performance Strategies, Ltd., a 30 - year old firm specializing in organizational development, training and executive coaching, primarily in financial services, pharmaceutical and entertainment firms.

The first member of her family to go to college, Lee holds an Ed.D. in Education Administration from Yeshiva University (NYC), an MA in Psychology from Manhattan College (NYC), and a B.A. in Mathematics from the College of Mt. St. Vincent (NYC).

LEE INNOCENTI

Leadership Lessons Learned Early

Looking back on my life's journey, I realize that the attitudes and skills I used in business I learned as a child. Once learned, these skills served to form a foundation upon which I would build other skills that carried me through all my relationships, both personal and professional. For example, with the help of wonderful mentors, I learned various business skills that, combined with earlier life lessons, gave me a set of "leadership skills" that helped me attain the top corporate position in my function. It is the awareness of lessons learned and layering one lesson on top of another that created a complex, nuanced set of behaviors that allowed for agile problem solving, regardless of the situation. Also, the support of many coworkers was an invaluable contribution to the development of my leadership skills.

I was five years old when I realized that I wanted to make as much money as possible. How? I set my mind to figure it out -- at FIVE! My parents never discussed money as they were not especially ambitious. But I sure was, and I began observing how my parents managed money. Mom had a shiny, blue tin box with eight compartments, each with its own labeled lid: rent, food, medical, savings, clothing, gifts, charity, and children's allowance. When we would go shopping, I would watch Mom go to the tin and take out what she needed. If one compartment was empty, after much deliberation, she would carefully take money from one compartment and move it to another. The savings compartment built up until the money went into the bank. Dad was the breadwinner in the family but Mom managed the money. I sensed women had power even then.

I received a small allowance for a series of tasks I had to complete. I had to make my bed each morning before going to school, empty the garbage, and wash or dry the dishes every night. Only on one occasion, when I was perhaps six or seven, I refused to make my bed and Mom warned me that she would charge my allowance if she was going to do my work. It was not clear to me what "charge" meant, but I still would not make my bed that day. At the end of the week, my allowance was ten cents short of the twenty-five cents I usually earned! I was shocked and annoyed but I liked the fairness of it and I never missed completing a task again. To this day, I budget my money and am a resolute saver. I learned responsibility early. I also learned that if I didn't work, I would not get paid. Later, as a manager, I used a consequences and rewards system to motivate resistant people. I was lucky to learn all of this at such a young age.

When I was five or six years old, I asked my Mom how I could increase my allowance. It's not that I needed the money, rather, I decided that money was a way to measure my productivity and I liked measuring my progress. I was always a very competitive child; I competed with myself if there was no one else to compete with. By this time, I had several piggy banks that mimicked Mom's tin box. Allowance and holiday monies were divided among my piggy banks. I had one for savings, one for family/gifts, one for college (I knew from this exercise that I would be going to college) and one piggy bank for me. I put 50% of my money into savings and divided the rest into thirds. I learned simple division and fractions! Mom said I could volunteer to do extra tasks around the house and I would be paid additional money. She, or I, would identify potential work opportunities and we would negotiate the pay for the extra tasks. Every day I looked for ways I could help and earn more. Cleaning the oven was big pay -- a dollar! Weeding the garden was less. I learned math, to show initiative, and negotiation skills all at once.

At about seven years old, I kept thinking of how to increase my revenue and decided to open a library in my basement for the local kids. The public library was at least 15 miles away and many parents were too busy to take their children there. I saw a perfect opportunity to meet a neighborhood need, and we always had an abundance of books. Kids could borrow my books for free but had to pay a daily penny late fee if they did not return the books on time. I prayed they would be late returning books. Running this library required crude record keeping or I would not be paid. So, I learned how to organize books and data at this early age. I also had an unpaid library assistant, a best friend who just wanted to do whatever I was doing. From this I learned that people will work to be part of a meaningful or fun project.

When I was 12 years old, I wanted to go on a trip with the Girl Scouts to Washington, DC. The cost was $25, and Mom said I could go if I earned the money; she would not pay. After much deliberation about what people would buy and what I could sell, I decided to make fashion pins out of flat toothpicks glued together, painted with leftover "paint by number" paint, and then embellished with the buyer's name made from alphabet soup letters. I charged twenty-five cents a pin. My grandmother, a supervisor of the AT&T phone cafeteria, placed my handmade marketing sign by the cash register and brought home orders every night. My girlfriend in another school was conscripted to sell my wares to her school friends, for which she was paid nothing; I did not know about pyramid marketing at that time! I made my $25 quickly and had extra money for trinkets on the trip. Only years later did I ever make it up to my girlfriend for all her efforts. I learned about marketing, sales, and production. It was clear I could not be a success without help from others.

As I got older, other schemes included a lemonade stand which I set up near our home where the trolley stopped, so thirsty travelers would be in ready supply. I learned about supply and demand. Mom packed the most wonderful lunches with sandwiches, candy, fruit, nuts, and veggies. If I felt full, I would sell some of this at lunch time. Homework came easily to me, and kids would ask me for answers so they would not have to do the work. I knew from early lessons that if someone else does your work, you were "charged", so the children I thought were smart enough to do the work themselves but were lazy, I charged for each answer. If I thought they were not capable, I gave away the answers. Unconsciously, I created my own crude kind of charity which I knew was important.

I came home one day and told my mom about Jan who had "cooties". No one liked her or would play with her. Mom made me imagine how Jan felt being treated this way. I resisted this because I did not want to be like Jan. Eventually, though, I could feel her immense sadness and self-loathing whenever she would hear such name calling. In the end, Mom suggested a play date with Jan to help her feel included. I worried that if the other kids found out, I would have cooties, too. I clearly remember Mom sitting next to me, supervising my call to Jan to invite her over after school. To my surprise, Jan was a lovely girl and we became friends. Her cooties went away and they did not rub off on me. I learned not to judge people and to have compassion for others. This memory still comes up for me as I navigate transactions with some less popular colleagues.

I began to read when I was four, as my parents read to me each night. I would point to the pictures and letters and try to decipher the symbols. One day, as the family gathered around on a Sunday afternoon, I read haltingly to my grandmother and everyone was so happy, and admired my achievement. I learned being good at schoolwork would get me much admiration and attention. I decided then that I would be the best in school whenever I finally enrolled.

My parents did not send us to summer camp. My Mother wanted to spend time with us in the summer. We would go away to the mountains with Dad for two weeks as a family. Otherwise, Mom amused us during the day. Mom and Dad were Catholic, as were Dad's parents. My Mom's mother worshiped at the Episcopalian church because her preferred Presbyterian church was too far away. Mom's father was Jewish, yet Mom enrolled us, with our Baptist friends, in a free Baptist summer camp because it had a bus to pick up and return the children each day. When I questioned why I was going to a camp of a different religion, Mom explained that it was all the same to God, and I should learn how people worship differently. That sounded good to me, and I loved every minute of it. To this day, I can still sing the songs we learned in this camp when I was, maybe, eight years old. I learned great acceptance and appreciation of various religions and I still study comparative religion.

My Supportive Family Unit

My sister, Beth, is three years older than me. We had a lovely childhood together, but, given the age difference, she had her friends and I had mine. Her choice was to be a housewife and she gave our family four lovely children and eight grandchildren. Her children provided me with many hours of being a loving aunt, which satisfied all my maternal needs.

I was the first college graduate in our immediate family. My maternal grandparents married young. My maternal grandmother did not finish high school and I am not sure if my maternal grandfather did. My wealthy, Orthodox Jewish, maternal grandfather, was disowned for marrying a Presbyterian woman, and he was denied any further education by his parents. He was, however, allowed to work in the family business of hardware stores, movie theaters, and catering. He eventually, painfully, abandoned his wife and children, leaving them penniless and out on the street after being evicted for nonpayment of rent. When my mom was 17 years old, she was horrified to find her furniture on the curb when she returned home from school one day. My grandfather was a nonperson in my life. My mom and her brother deprived him of ever knowing his grandchildren, and from the day he left the house, they had nothing to do with him. In those days, there were no requirements for alimony or child support. To support the family, my grandmother went to work as a waitress in a tea shop until she moved to the AT&T cafeteria where she worked her way up from the kitchen to supervisor of the employee dining room.

My grandmother was fifth or sixth generation American with English, French Canadian, and American Indian heritage, with English traditions being dominant. My grandfather was of Russian and Hungarian descent and was second generation American. These grandparents were from Yonkers, NY. Though I did not know my grandfather, I did meet his siblings who were wonderful, and we developed a warm friendship when I was in my twenties. I learned that spouses can abandon you, that there are big disappointments in life, and that I'd best have a backup plan of self-sufficiency.

My Catholic, paternal grandparents were from Italy. At 13 years of age, my grandfather, Nono, having left behind his entire family in Florence, arrived in boat steerage and headed to Michigan to be with distant relatives. I assume he left Italy because there was no work or food, but I am not sure. He worked as a coal miner until he lost his eye due to a mining accident. My grandmother, Nona, landed on Ellis Island with her abandoned mother when she was 18 years old; they arrived from Primaluna (near Lake Como). She, too, headed to Michigan where there were relatives. My grandmother worked as a maid and her mother as a seamstress. Her father had left the family to find work in Argentina but never returned. We have no idea what happened to him. Neither my grandmother nor grandfather went beyond 6th grade in school, yet they could both read and write in two languages (Italian and English). Together, even during the Great Depression in the late 1930s, they were able to buy two homes by means of extreme penny-pinching, and funds from taking in boarders. I knew them as apartment building superintendents in later years. I learned to take pride in the immigrant experience which reinforced working hard and saving money as principles to live by.

Seeing two families abandoned by breadwinners, forcing uneducated women to survive on their own by working for low wages, I vowed I would be well educated and always be able to support myself. I would depend upon NO ONE for my food or shelter.

My mom graduated high school but turned down a college scholarship since she had to go to work to help support her family. My Dad also graduated high school and was a successful salesman who ultimately quit his job after more than 20 years because his firm wanted him to travel and Dad would not leave my Mom at night. I learned that family always comes first.

As a salesman, my Dad had to submit expense reports every week to his company, and I would ride with him to the post office every Sunday when he submitted his report. He explained to me that though he was a successful salesman, his expenses were lower than those of the other salesmen. When I asked why, he explained that many business people falsely added extra expenses to their report so they could have more money refunded to them; that was dishonest -- a form of stealing. I learned expense reports were an indication of integrity in business. When I lost one of my hard contact lenses, I suggested to Dad that he use the insurance he had purchased for my lenses so that he would not have to buy me a new lens. He explained the insurance was for “damaged” lenses, not lost ones, even though the insurance company would never know the difference. He explained that this, too, would be dishonest. I learned integrity was a very big deal in life and it was better to spend money in order to preserve your honesty.

My parents and grandparents were my first mentors who gave me life lessons. The women in my family were strong, hardworking, capable matriarchs of the family. In those days, most women did not work outside of the home, so all the working women in my family were pathfinders ahead of me who inspired me to find a career instead of merely finding jobs. The men in my family (except one grandfather and perhaps one great-grandfather) were very loving of their women and children, supportive of the family unit, and willing to let the women manage the household. My Dad was so proud of me. He cheered for each childhood achievement, and attended every school event. He taught me sports and played with me outside. We were pals and I loved him dearly. It was my Mom, however, who, day after day, actively attended to my every challenge and event, and did all the disciplining of us children. I love her deeply, too. I liked seeing women in an equal position with men, if only in the home. Today Mom is 103 and lives with me; she is still my best friend.

High School Success

As I made my way through school, I discovered, to my dismay, that I was not the sharpest knife in the drawer. I was popular and in the top 10% of my classes. But, I had to work harder than the really smart kids to get the same good grades. I enjoyed working hard but it stung, given my out-sized ambition, to realize that I was not, nor would I ever be, number 1. I learned that I needed to work harder than most to get ahead or just achieve the same results. I was disappointed with my raw, native intelligence but satisfied with my achievements thus far, so I didn't know what to think of myself. Oddly, I won many academic awards in school even though my grades were not the best. I asked some teachers why they awarded the prize to me when clearly someone else had achieved better performance in class. They explained that I was an enthusiastic learner, willing to help others and that counted as much as the actual academic achievement. I learned that passion and helping others can differentiate performance.

By the time I got to high school, my lessons learned enabled me to be elected for various leadership roles, such as vice president of our sorority, participant in school plays, editor of the school paper and leader of various team events. I suspect it was because I completed what was required, worked hard, always respected people's feelings, never missed a deadline, thanked people profusely for their help, made projects fun, and was honest in my transactions. I donated my time for various charities, like working as a volunteer in a hospital, to fulfill my need to help others. The principles I learned early were paying off.

I did not win any big scholarship, reinforcing that I was not as smart as I'd hoped. I was awarded a small scholarship which made me feel better. I had good grades and would get accepted by many colleges, but my parents could not afford tuition and room and board. Neither my parents nor I wanted to take on college loans; accumulating debt was shunned in my family. Since they could afford tuition only, I became a day-hop to a small Catholic college (College of Mount Saint Vincent), in the Bronx, NY. It was well known locally but not outside a 150-mile radius; nor was it competitive with any Ivy League schools. I spent those four years studying very hard to demonstrate my gratitude to my parents for their investment in me. I would go out on dates only on Saturday nights because I studied the rest of the time. I graduated with a 3.35 GPA which was the best I could achieve, even with all my diligent studying. In defense of my GPA, I had to take religion, philosophy, and Italian -- a total of 16 classes! I competed with first generation Italian girls who went to Catholic school, and were fluent in both religion and language. I did not stand a chance as a public school kid and these required courses brought my average down. The day I graduated was the last day I took money from my father, as I now knew that I would be a very good earner, even if I wasn't sure how. I was ready for independence.

Early Career Advice

My parents' greatest hope was that I would achieve more than they had, which was much more than their parents had. We were "upwardly mobile." They knew of only two careers where women were well regarded: nursing and teaching. They honestly knew of no other professional jobs open to women. I, too, had no idea there might be other options as the few, professional women we knew were teachers. Computer classes, which were brand new in my college, were closed to women; it was deemed that women would never have a technical career. The sight of blood frightened me, so I opted, reluctantly, for teaching as a career. I majored in mathematics, which I loved, and education. I graduated qualified to teach K-6 or 7-12 in mathematics. I thought two options for work would double my chances of employment. With a full-time job as a public school teacher in the Yonkers, NY system, I pursued a Master's of Psychology degree at Manhattan College, also in the Bronx, NY. I thought having the option of being a counselor would be a third option I could add to my career possibilities. I graduated as a licensed psychologist.

I got my first taste of leadership as an adult when the school superintendent selected me to join the "high potential" group of future administrators. Though I loved the children, we were in the middle of integrating the schools and the parents were rabid. Also, the school system was bankrupt, making it hard to get even pencils for children. We experienced four strikes in seven years (by teachers, administrators, custodians, and secretaries). It was very hard to teach before, during, and after the strikes that represented months of time out of the school year. I taught for only three years and was promoted to the Human Relations function (helping teachers and students figure out how to work with one another) before I went into business.

Don, my supervisor in the school system, became my first mentor, when amid stiff competition, I was selected to join his Human Resource Department. He taught me the craft of organizational development and training adults. Don was fabulous; the best Organizational Development/Training professional I have ever seen. For three years he gave me feedback EVERY single day, for a minimum of 30 minutes. No detail of my behavior was exempt from his discerning eye: my body language, my clothing, the timber of my voice, my choice of words, key points I was making, and my pedagogical methods were all grist for the mill. I listened with rapt attention to his advice, learned what a gift feedback was, and developed my technical skills while I pursued my EdD at night. Because Don was outspoken about being African American, I began to have all African American friends for a few years. Learning about this culture was both fascinating and heartbreaking: "No, we don't trust white people, not even you." Don also sent me to many external workshops to learn about myself, my behavior, and my motivations. I started reading metaphysical books to try to understand what my purpose should be in this life, but I did not find the answer at that time. I was Don's shadow, his clone; with his care and feeding I grew very rapidly. He crafted state of the art interventions to help the children, teachers, and parents integrate and I could see changes in the behavior of children, parents, and teachers after working with us. We were having an effect. Don left the school system to go into business, leaving me in tears and to find my own way. I decided that I, too, must leave and go into business. I would follow in his footsteps and secure a job in business, but in a different company.

Business Mentors Were All Around

In a school system, many women are administrators (school management staff). They earn the same salary as their male counterparts. I had heard it was different in business. I now needed business mentors to help me navigate and understand this new environment and I found several devoted, caring men to help me.

I started as an Organizational Development/Training specialist for Automatic Data Processing. In the beginning, I had no idea how I would find my voice, be heard, and be invited into important discussions. We had more than 100 regional offices that were profit centers. These profit centers received a report card every month on about 20 dimensions that were published worldwide to all management, with a winner declared for the month. Always looking for a way to measure my contribution, I thought if I could improve one or more of the criteria on the report card, I would add value to the business. In the company, women in leadership positions were rare, and I knew I had to earn entry into the "boys club" by demonstrating that I could help their business. With my staff, we started doing team interventions around the country, and to our surprise and delight, the offices where we worked always won the award for the month's best overall performance and continued to perform well thereafter. I had found a way to demonstrate competence that the men would acknowledge as very helpful. Thereafter, I was admitted to senior level meetings with relative ease. I had found my voice and my team's voice in this predominantly male company.

The company was very proud of itself when it made me the first corporate female vice president. I was thrilled, and my coworkers seemed genuinely happy for me. My corner office was huge, and seemingly, too big for someone like me. I moved my desk where coworkers walking by could not see me in this large office, lest anyone realize I really did not belong in such a lofty space. Did I deserve this title? Was I a fraud? I wasn't sure. In the meantime, I made sure that when you walked by my office you could only see the important visitors, and I hoped observers would wonder who owned this office to attract such august people. It took me about a year to rearrange my office so that my desk was again visible. I learned many women felt this way as they started to achieve success.

I now needed no mentor for my craft, as Don was so thorough, and I could grow in my technical skills through various seminars and conferences. I was not prepared for the politics of business, and did not understand how it all worked. Here I needed much help. Various executives asked me if I ever played sports. What? In those days, there were NO intramural sports for girls, only cheerleading or twirling. What did this have to do with leading? My first business supervisor, Bernie, was a very talented executive who seemed to be able to get anything approved and was liked by everyone. His staff, including me, adored him. We would do anything for him, and I was inspired to be just like him. I decided he would be my mentor who would decipher sports questions and all things political for me.

I watched him in meetings, going toe to toe with other men. While I admired his guts and fast thinking, I instinctively knew that, as a woman, I could not behave the same way he did; at times he used profanity, raised his voice, or was threatening. Yet, there were no women executives to guide me. Bernie and I had many discussions about how to influence people in the organization. I listened and watched carefully, picking out bits of behavior I thought I could use.

Cleverly, I thought, I will use my staff to train me on how to be a good manager and leader, while also developing their technical skills. Every six months, the newest team member would gather anonymous data, which is a skill, from all my staff, a few peers, and my supervisor. After, he or she would consolidate the data (a skill) and prepare a professional report for me to share with my supervisor (a skill). Lastly, he or she would deliver the feedback to me (a skill) and, then, deliver the feedback to my staff and me in a joint meeting (a skill). Admittedly, I was often disappointed with my feedback, as I hoped I was so much better than what the report said. However, I could not deny the examples proffered. I enlisted my team and my supervisor to help me improve some specific leadership/management behaviors of mine during the next six months and they were empowered to give me feedback anytime about my behavior -- and they did! I did this twice a year for many years. Not only was I becoming a better leader, but my staff was becoming better at their craft, too. Life was so good. I was passionate about my job, my staff, and my company. I was learning to lead by following advice from my team. Individuals may be wrong about something, but rarely is the entire group wrong. My staff became my loud, vocal compass. Constant feedback was the lifeblood of success.

Along the way, after each major project, I asked for feedback from my stakeholders. I listened carefully to how I, and my team, could improve and how we could be more effective. Bernie would weigh in with his opinions on my competence, and I always had a set of goals to achieve for the department and for him. There were layoffs in the company over the years, and people were threatened with losing their job, though I was rather sanguine about not being let go. Bernie assured me my job security was in my skill set, my reputation, and my network. And he believed that, were I to be eliminated, I would land somewhere good. So I did not lose sleep over cutbacks. I imbued my staff with the same sense of confidence in themselves. We were never let go. After working many years together, Bernie retired and I was again bereft of a "godfather" figure.

I enjoyed working with my next supervisor for two years. He was very politically supportive of my initiatives but was recruited away to another firm. My third boss, to my dismay, was devoid of integrity or a moral compass. I found him grossly cheating on his expense report, blaming his wonderful secretary every time he was late for a meeting, and lying when it served him. To remain silent would have been the politically correct thing to do, but I could not let him think that we were all so stupid that we did not notice his lapses of integrity and moral judgment. When I confronted him on his expense report and verbal abuse of his secretary (she was an icon of efficiency and effectiveness), I knew I was deciding my fate. I would not work for someone I did not respect and, therefore, would leave this company I loved to start my own business. It was time for my services to produce revenue for my own consulting firm, instead of being an "expense" to a firm. During those eleven years I had learned:

1. You can work people hard, but you must never deny them their dignity.
2. A successful termination is when the employee is able to say, "Thank you for helping me leave a place where I do not fit in."
3. Caring for the whole employee (their family, health, career, and emotional well-being) is critical to gaining their loyalty.
4. A manager may be best friends with her employees, but must maintain a position of respect and leadership.
5. Honesty is paramount in all dialogue; it allows one to speak about her feelings and thoughts authentically in small or large group settings.

6. If you are going to do something that might harm a person's career, you must warn them. Invite them to the meeting where the matter will be discussed so that they have an opportunity to make a defense. As an example, I had a 50-year-old, married, purchasing vice president who was having an affair with his new secretary; she was 25 years old. The problem was not the affair per se. The problem was that he was falsifying her time card so that they could have long, leisurely lunches, take three-day weekends, and travel overseas on business trips without his professional staff. The 15 other young, professional women working for him were furious about his duplicity and that he awarded perks based on sexual relations. The young women told me of their plan to discuss his affair with his wife. They would also initiate a class action lawsuit if he didn't end the time card fraud and if he didn't stop awarding perks unfairly. I was hired to improve team relationships. My concern was that once the women coalesced, they might bring this action against the company for discrimination. I showed the VP three pages of examples of illegal and inappropriate behavior with his secretary. He admitted the allegations were true but, shockingly,

he refused to modify his behavior! I explained to him that his behavior put our large, international, and well-known retail company at risk for a lawsuit. I asked him if he wanted to be present when I discussed the information with Corporate. I explained that my intent was not to harm him, but to protect the company from a lawsuit initiated by his staff and to create a well-functioning team. As a consultant, I had knowledge of a possible class action lawsuit being brought against the company, and I was obligated to share that fact with corporate staff so that they could mitigate the situation. Together, we set a meeting date, and I related to him the exact information I would present to Corporate so that he could prepare his defense. While we never became best friends, he had a chance to defend himself before Corporate, my integrity was left intact, and the lawsuit was avoided. In the end, the VP was moved to a different role with no direct reports, and a new VP was brought in to take over the department and restore integrity. The secretary was reassigned and ultimately, they married a few years later.

7. If you generously acknowledge your team's contribution to the department's accomplishments, privately and publicly, the team

solidifies and team members' political value increases. Basically, your employees will shine, and you will glow in their light.

8. Promote your best employees, even though you will hate losing them. Having these valuable advocates for you operating throughout the organization will make negotiating various items throughout the company easier for you in the long run.
9. A competent team is essential. Help poor performers to improve or let them go. Allowing poor performers to linger helps no one, least of all yourself.
10. You owe employees direct, specific feedback for every performance, good or bad. Employees should also be reviewed twice a year, whether mandated or not.
11. If you can't offer advancement yourself, be a part of your employees' career development planning, even if that means encouraging them to leave the company to work for the competition.
12. If you can't be loyal to your supervisor, look for work under a different supervisor or leave. You shouldn't work for someone you can't support.

Jumping Off the Cliff with a Parachute

ADP was reorganizing and I saw an opportunity to leave gracefully. I offered to resign, along with some of my staff, if we were given generous severance packages. My unpleasant supervisor was eager to bring in his own people who would ignore his transgressions, and he quickly agreed to make a deal with me. He even threw in more money if I could get my sick employee to leave with me. We were jubilant with our generous severance packages.

I had kept an "alumni" list of executives who had left the company in the previous four years, and thought I would start my own consulting firm with these alumni as potential clients. Many were now presidents of Fortune 500 companies, heads of Human Resources, and vice presidents of various operations departments. Before my last day at ADP, I had secured 100 days of consulting work with one client, and I had my severance package. So my transition, though scary, was financially secure; at least for the first two years.

Selling was new to me. Now my job was to figure out what services to market, what my unique service proposition would be, market my services, find work, sign deals, develop consulting materials for training programs or organizational development interventions, deliver the programs, and, on the weekends, do all the administrative work. 80-hour work weeks were the norm and I loved it. There was no work-life balance. My supportive husband had his own business and was busy working crazy hours too. We both traveled. Our weekend rendezvous were exciting and sustaining. Mutually, we agreed that a life with no children would suit us both and allow us to focus on our beloved work.

Clients referred their friends to me; I was passed from one friend to another, gaining clients and growing revenue. As my firm grew, some of my previous employees from ADP joined us. So I could again work, travel the world, and have fun with my dear friends, while we supported ourselves very well. My focus was financial service firms, pharmaceuticals, and entertainment -- money, drugs, and rock and roll. Everything I learned up to this point I used to grow and sustain my business. In the first twenty-five years, I did not have one unsold consulting day. Sometimes I would be so weary from work, but I always knew I was lucky to have found my niche.

My Purpose Finally Revealed

Many years after I left ADP, former female colleagues called me to catch up. To my surprise, each referred to me as her mentor. I had done no such thing that I was aware of. All those times that I had lunch, coffee, or took phone calls from mostly younger women, discussing their business dilemmas, they saw as mentoring. I saw it as just being a friend. It is true that anyone who wanted some help or advice could always get some of my time. To this day, I spend about two hours a week helping others, which is a huge source of satisfaction and joy for me. Just a little bit, I like to think, I help the world turn. Now that I am semi-retired, I find myself helping the children of my former colleagues and clients with their resumés, their networking, or their job-hunting process. No one makes it in business without significant help. I have been blessed.

Lee, Grandmother, and sister Beth

Lee, Beth and their Father

Lee and Jan

Lee and Bernie

Lee and her Mother

Typical executive offsite.

AMY LIEBSCHUTZ LONDON

Raised in Cincinnati Ohio in a musical family, Amy London followed her (mother's) dream to New York City and abroad to establish her powerful career as a jazz singer, performer and teacher. Well-respected by the jazz community around the globe, Amy developed music programs and teaches jazz in New York City and in jazz camps all over the world.

An Alpha to the core, Amy raised her family while juggling the demands of a performing career under the bright lights, mostly in New York. A brilliant networker whose courage on stage is truly remarkable, Amy sang with her sisters growing up and earned a music degree from Syracuse University before embarking on her stage career.

POUND ON!!

AMY LIEBSCHUTZ LONDON

Dispelling The Myth Of The Chick Singer

I was born a chick singer, there was no avoiding it. Music was pervasive in my house when I arrived. I am the youngest of 3 daughters, and my Mom's family was and still is full of musicians. My Mom, Edith Leshner, was a radio actress in the 1940s and played piano. My Mom's youngest brother, Uncle Gene, at 90 plus, is still a tenor sax player, and in his youth traveled with the Ray Anthony and Johnny Long Big Bands. My Mom's second youngest brother, Uncle Don, was a jazz DJ and voiceover actor. I even heard his most famous commercial in NYC in the early 90s, "Kahn's Wieners: The Weiner The World Awaited!" Mom's older brother, my Uncle Saul, sang songs. His big hit was "I Left My Heart In San Francisco" with which he regaled us with at every holiday.

He also told jokes a la Henny Youngman. All 5 of my Uncle Saul's kids are professional or amateur musicians. My elder sister Linda is a professional singer, who was the first call choral alto in San Fransisco throughout the 80s, 90s and 00s, and is on a variety of early music recordings from those years, with the San Francisco Symphony Chorus, American Bach Soloists, Arvo Paert, and others. My middle sister Patty possesses little singing talent, and certainly never pursued music professionally like Linda and I did. The joke amongst the 3 of us is, my email is amylondonsings, Linda's is liebsings, and Patty's is patdontsing!

My Dad, David Liebschutz, always claimed to be tone deaf, and that there was no musical talent on his side at all, except that his Uncle Harry improvised on the organ at the movie theaters for Silent Films. Perhaps that is the only glimmer of musical talent on his side.

I am on the tail end of the Baby Boomers, born into a very comfortable middle class Jewish family in Cincinnati, Ohio. My maternal Grandma, Anna Leshner (nee Sonya Vogel) was a refugee from the Ukraine, and barely survived the ethnic cleansing of Jews that was happening around the turn of the century in Russia.

At the age of 14 or 15, her parents booked her passage on a ship to Ellis Island, probably around 1910, and she was orphaned the moment she said goodbye to them, much like the scene in 'Fiddler on the Roof,' when Hodel sings 'Far From The Home I Love' and says goodbye to her father Tevye and her little shtetl, then boards a train to Siberia to join her husband, Perchik. The difference is that instead of joining Perchik the Revolutionary at a gulag, Grandma Anna came to New York City, lived briefly with her half brother Max Vogel in the Bronx, and worked at a sweat shop in Lower Manhattan.

Grandma Anna did not like busy, crowded NYC, or working in a sweat shop, so she traveled to Cincinnati to become the cleaning woman for her wealthy cousins, the Safers. There she met my Grandfather Sam Leshner, also a refugee from Russia. He was born in Kiev, and probably emigrated around the same time as Grandma, but was luckier: he and his 3 brothers and a sister made it safely to Ohio, and were actually able to go back to Kiev and later bring their mother to America.

Grandma's maiden name was Sonia Vogel, and it was changed at Ellis Island, like so many others, to Anna Vogel.

Grandpa Sam's real last name was Leschtiner, thus Leshner in America. Grandma and Grandpa were very poor, but very happy. They settled in rural Hamilton, Ohio, just half an hour outside of Cincinnati, in a house in the country that probably looked a lot more like Grandma's shtetl in Komenetz Poldolsk than the tenements of New York City did.

Grandma had a beautiful, naturally operatic voice. My memories of her are wonderful; she was so sweet, so loving, always so happy to see all of us. She made her incredible butter cookies so often that her hands always smelled like butter. She would caress my face and say, "Shayne punim" and kiss me. She is so beloved in our family, that all 4 of our girls, my two daughters, and Linda's two daughters, are named after her: Linda's Shoshanna and Amara, my Sofia and Anna.

Grandma Anna never learned to read or write English, but she was a wizard of a homemaker. She never once made a mistake at the grocery store, she made delicious matzo ball soup, gefilte fish from scratch for Passover, and the aforementioned cookies as well as a wonderful honey cake for Rosh Hashanah. She was always in the kitchen singing as she cooked. When my Mom was a teen, she and Grandma used to go to downtown Cincinnati, look in the fancy dress shop windows, my Mom would choose what she liked, and Grandma would go home and make the clothing for her from scratch, no pattern.

Grandpa Sam had a gorgeous high baritone voice, and was a well-trained Yeshiva boy. In shule, he would stand next to the rabbi and sing the entire torah and haftorah, like a cantor, even though by trade he was a used car salesman. Grandma and Grandpa Leshner were poor, but they had a loving, happy family. In my memory, Grandma never spoke about the horrors she witnessed when Jews around her in her village were being slaughtered. She was just happy all the time, and no doubt so grateful to have this beautiful family, and food on the table. The only thing she complained about was that Grandpa Sam was constantly bringing strangers home to eat at their house; he had so much empathy for those struggling, and this was during the Depression.

My Dad's parents were descendants of German refugees that arrived in Cincinnati in 1851, when there was a huge influx of Germans to Ohio and all over the midwest, both Jewish and non-Jewish. To this day, you can still look in the phone book in

Cincinnati, and see a lot of German names. My Dad's ancestors, Leon Safdi, from Egypt, and Carolyn Bertelheimer, from Germany, were married in Cincinnati in the mid 1800s. My Dad was a merchant, like so many of his friends, and as was typical for a successful Jewish businessman, he was in the 'shmata' business. He owned a string of high end women's clothing stores in Cincinnati, called 'Martins' Town and Country.' (He certainly wasn't going to call the stores 'Liebschutz's!'.) His family, having lived there for several generations, was able to establish itself financially as successful merchants. He was not a first generation child. Instead, his father gave him a millinery store (hat and gloves) to run when he was only sixteen years old.

When my Dad met my Mom, a beautiful svelte gal I refer to as a 'Jewish fox,' she became a living model for his fashions, along with her two sisters-in-law, and thus began our family: A first generation pretty Jewish woman married to a successful businessman, and a very comfortable home in a comfortable neighborhood. We weren't super rich, nor were we super spoiled, but we lacked for nothing.

TV and record players were very big in our house. We grew up in the era of Ed Sullivan, The Flintstones, Patty Duke, The Twilight Zone, Bewitched, etc. In the mail we regularly received newly marketed convenience food samples from Proctor and Gamble, which was the big industry in Cincinnati, (think 1 2 3 Jell-O, Velveeta cheese and SpaghettiOs. Serious junk food!) There were two cars in every driveway, pink and turquoise kitchens were the norm, and a piano in every living room. The piano was in the house before I was born. Baldwin Piano Company was based in Cincinnati, and we had a Baldwin Acrosonic Upright piano, which I still have in my home today. I am very sentimentally attached to it. When we were little girls, my Mom had a favorite song, "Forest of the Flowers," that she would play and we would skip and dance around the living room. She also played "Body and Soul." And that was about it. She never practiced, and as the years went by she would lose a few bars of this, a few bars of that, always complaining that she couldn't do it anymore, but never willing to practice to retain it.

Dad was a very distant personality, perhaps a typical post WW II man. He was fiscally responsible, but left the child rearing and home keeping to Mom. He came home from work every night at 10:00 p.m., and Mom always had to make a second dinner just for him. He had no idea how to deal with a house full of noisy, mouthy, opinionated little girls, so he basically shut us out. I know that he meant well, but after two failed marriages, I know that my lack of any kind of emotional connection to my Dad had a huge impact on my ability to choose the right partners. It is only now, in my early 60s, and after decades of therapy, that I have finally figured out how to ask for what I need in a relationship, that I can't fix what was wrong with the relationship with my father, and also how to avoid the wrong types of men.

My Mom overcompensated for our lack of any relationship with our Dad, and for his explosive temper. We were generally afraid of him; at 6' 3" he was quite an imposing and sometimes frightening figure. If we ever needed anything from him, Mom was our filter. As I said, she came from this raucous, funny, fun loving musical family. She was an actress and pianist in her youth, and as a teen she was the star of the dramas in her high school. She used to love to tell us how she was the character actress in Clifford Odet's "Waiting for Lefty." She was so good at pulling off a Brooklyn accent, that one day, in the stall in the girls' bathroom at her high school, she overheard some younger girls talking about her, wondering if she really was from Brooklyn and talked like that! She was so proud of that. After high school, from the late 1930s through the 40s, my Mom was in a quartet of actors who performed live on the radio every Friday night. It must have been such a thrill for my grandparents and uncles to turn on the radio and hear her weekly. No doubt she was a small town celebrity in Hamilton, Ohio.

So this was the atmosphere that formed me: A fun loving, beautiful warm and funny Mom who took care of everything, a distant but successful father, the most adorable, sweet and wonderful Russian immigrant grandparents who adored us, and spoke Yiddish as their first language. My Dad's mother, Goldie, was wonderful and loving, and unfortunately died of cancer when I was only 5. Dad's father Leon was generally grumpy and nasty, and Dad told us that when he was a little boy, he was not allowed to speak at the dinner table.

Grandpa Leon, who had to be 5' 5" at the most, had an enormous appetite and was round as a globe. He had a white mustache, a ring of white hair around his bald head, and always wore those super high waisted men's pants, I remember he favored brown pants, with a thin brown leather belt and a white shirt tucked in. He looked like a cross between Humpty Dumpty and a globe, his belt the circumference between the northern and southern hemispheres. How he fathered 3 tall, slender good looking men is beyond me, and Grandma was a saint - it certainly wasn't the mailman! I remember Mom always had him over for Sunday dinners; he lived 10 years past Grandma Goldie. One Sunday dinner while we were eating, I remember him making a snide comment about my big appetite. I regret to this day that I didn't have the chutzpah to say, "Gee, Grandpa, I wonder who I inherited it from!!" But I was about 8, and generally terrified of him.

I had my own room in our house as a kid, and my own bathroom, too. It was the smallest of 4 bedrooms, as the youngest child usually gets the smallest room. Considering the attached bathroom, I probably was living in the maid's room. I was a girly girl, my bedroom was pink, and I was probably OCD, the neatest child anyone could imagine. I was so obsessive compulsive about tidiness, that my underwear, socks and wardrobe were color coded, and I used to line my stuffed animals along the wall, and kiss them each good night, every night.

But other than this extraordinary neatness, which from a psychological view was probably my attempt to maintain control in a somewhat dysfunctional, chaotic household, the MOST important thing in my room was my clock radio. I had that radio on constantly, and sang along with it and memorized songs from birth. When I was two years old, my favorite songs were 'Johnny Angel' and 'I Wanna be Bobby's Girl.' A few years later, my two older sisters, Patty and Linda and I watched the Beatles' debut performance on the Ed Sullivan show, jumping up and down on my parents' bed and witnessing this historic performance on their black and white Zenith TV. At the age of 6, I was harmonizing with Linda, age 12, as she played guitar and sang folk songs of the day. At the age of 8, I began reading music, and I was probably the only kid in 3rd grade who loved playing the recorder, and being in choir. I also began piano lessons at age 8, and I was reading music in choir all the way through high school. I am one of the lucky Americans who grew up in a time when serious music was still cherished and well supported in the public school system. I have been reading music since age 8, and between that and my piano skills, I developed musical ability at a very early age.

At age 12, one day my sister Patty brought home Laura Nyro's Eli and the 13th Confession. I absolutely flipped out when I heard it. I still have that scratched LP that I played constantly for years. Up until that time, I was a decent pianist for my age, and singing in choir. Thanks to Laura, I discovered how to sing and express myself as a solo singer. Fortunately, some wise music book publisher released a songbook of 4 of her records and my Mom bought it for me. That dog-eared copy is still on my piano. Thanks to my sight-reading abilities at the piano, I was able to play through Laura's entire repertoire and play the arrangements on the piano that were very close to what she played on her recordings. For some reason, I was able to imitate her voice pretty accurately. Every single day after school, I would come home, and sit at the piano for a few hours, playing her music and singing my heart out.

Laura Nyro is a combination of many elements that spoke to me at the time. She was a prodigy that grew up in the Bronx in a house of left wing Jews. Her aunt turned her on to opera, but she was also very heavily influenced by a cappella singing, and would hang out in the subways and sing in groups with her friends when she was growing up. She was also very influenced by jazz. There is a very famous photo of Miles Davis hanging out with her at her recording session at Columbia records in the late 60s. Laura was half Eastern European Jewish/half Italian, she had a full figure and long flowing black hair. She described herself floating around NYC in her long skirts and hippy blouses, writing songs about what she saw and observed on the streets. She went to Music and Art High school, and before she graduated, she had already written some hits, such as Wedding Bell Blues and Stoned Soul Picnic, which were hits for the Fifth Dimension, and Stoney End, a hit for Barbra Streisand, And When I Die, a hit for Three Dog Night. She was so successful in her late teens and early 20s that she retired from the music business in her mid 20s. She was a pure artist, so brilliant and such a soulful singer, she hated the business and moved out of the city to a house in the countryside in Connecticut. We unfortunately lost her in 1996, she died from Ovarian Cancer at age 49, same as her mother.

During my teen angst years, Laura's soulfulness and deeply expressive, powerful voice answered all the loneliness and insecurity

I was experiencing. I never felt like I was one of the pretty girls, but I always knew that I could sing circles around anyone. Thanks to my innate musical talent, the fact that I was surrounded by a musical family, and growing up in the feminist era, with such female musical heroes as Laura Nyro, Joni Mitchell and Carole King, I found an identity that not only determined my entire adult life, but gave me the confidence that I needed to feel good about myself.

Growing up in the 60s and 70s was such a mixed bag: there were the civil rights and feminist movements, which were such a strong influence on me. I don't know if it was my lively, verbose and funny Mom's family, or if it was the feistiness of the times, but I have been an outspoken, opinionated gal since childhood. I remember standing on my teacher's desk in 8th grade, giving a speech about Women's Liberation, while the boys threw paper airplanes at each other in the back of the room. I remember putting on a black armband as a little girl, and marching in protests against the Vietnam War. I walked the 8 miles to school on Earth Day to save on auto exhaust.

Even though my Dad was emotionally vacant, he always supported our endeavors to achieve. He was, in his own way, an early male feminist. There were several female shop owners on his side of the family in Cincinnati, his first cousin Roz Epstein was one of the first doctors in her community, having become a doctor in the 1930's. My Dad was very proud of the fact that he attended the ordination of the first woman rabbi in America, Sally Priesand. Rabbi Priesand was ordained in 1972 at our Reform Jewish Synagogue, Plum Street Temple, a stunning Moorish style architectural masterpiece on the National Historic Landmark Registry, built in 1865.

On the flip side was the constant pressure in our family to look good and be junior models of the fashions of Martins', Dad's store. The three of us couldn't have rebelled more against that concept. First of all, Linda and I were not born tall and skinny, even though middle sister Patty is tall and skinny, so any kind of modeling was out for me. Considering the fact that Patty has been a card carrying communist her entire life, she could not have rebelled more against being a junior model for Martins'.

I always refer to my parents as 'Jewish Mad Men.' They hung out with other good looking, successful Jewish couples. The wives were all housewives, no career women, and they were all perfect looking, thin, fashionable. They all went out together every Saturday night, the men smoking their cigars, the women with their weekly visits to the beauty parlor, big diamond rings and fur coats.

My sisters and I, at very early ages, made a decision to not grow up and be that way. We all escaped from that insular world as soon as we could. Linda became a hippie the moment she went to college, Patty moved out in 11th grade, and I couldn't wait to get away from that stifling environment. I always had friends of all colors, religions and sexual orientation, and I was drawn to the jazz world as a 12 year old. Aside from the spectacular music, the jazz community is open to all people, regardless of race or religion.

The other big influence in media at that time was Twiggy, and the mod movement from London. Twiggy was a freak of nature, no doubt she was anorexic to maintain that look. The entire pop/op art, mod movement was pervasive in those days, all over the covers of Glamour and Seventeen magazine, on TV, everywhere you could find ads and commercials. As impressionable young women, these images of tall skinny Twiggy and others that looked like her were seared in our brains. Being born into a zoftig Jewish family, where big boobs and big, child bearing, bales-of-hay-lifting hips were the norm, this was an impossible image to match physically, and caused so many of us in our generation to develop serious body dysmorphia problems.

As a result, and also because the message the 3 of us got from our father that we were not pretty and that we were too fat, I had little confidence in my physical attractiveness. Granted all this, I really was a beautiful child, but I always felt ugly.

Mix all of this together, rebelling against the status quo of the model woman, the hippie and revolutionary movements and the arrival on the scene of Laura Nyro, Shirley Chisolm and Gloria Steinem, the outcome was what I became: a really great singer. I knew that even though I wasn't the prettiest or thinnest girl in my high school, but I could sing circles around just about every other girl in the school.

My main identity in high school became the girl who could sing and play like Laura Nyro and Carole King, and I was also an accomplished choral singer, making my way into the elite Walnut

Hills High School 16 Voice Ensemble. Naturally, when applying to colleges, I decided I wanted to be a professional singer and majored in voice in college. My parents naively said ok, they never once gave me that 'Don't you think you should major in music education?" speech. I honestly think they figured that, like my Mom, I would perform a little bit, and then move back to Cincinnati and marry some nice, rich Jewish doctor or lawyer.

However, this rebellious, smart, talented mouthy gal was having none of that. My Mom shipped me and my sister off to Dr. Sidney Peerless, the plastic surgeon who did all the Jewish girls' nose jobs in Cincinnati, the minute the 3 of us got our periods. Mom was gorgeous, and had a big nose, and was always kvetching about her nose. The 3 of us were brainwashed that our noses were ugly, so off I went at 15 for my nose job. By the time I got to college, always a place where one can start over and redefine, I had a little fake shiksa nose, long blonde hair, and learned how to do my makeup, instead of looking like a hippie all the time.

I flourished in college. I sang with bands the entire time I was there, was in several musicals and the lead in 'Candide' my senior year. I was a musical theatre major my Freshman year, but got out after I saw how the talent deficient skinny bottle blonde Barbie Doll types got cast in plays and I did not, because they were sleeping with the drama director, or looked like soap opera stars. Funny, that is still so much in play in show biz today.

I had a wonderful voice teacher, classical bass baritone Donald Miller. I stuck with him all 4 years at college. The first thing I learned was Bel Canto singing, a method of singing developed by Italians 500 years ago that is the basis for voice lessons globally. Mr. Miller helped me develop my opera sound. I started off with the classic 'Caro Mio Ben' everybody's first song - a love song in Italian from the 17th century. I fell in love with the Italian language, took two years of Italian Language in college, and spent my junior Spring semester in Florence, Italy. This was a life changing experience. Once I learned that I could get by in a foreign country all by myself, and speak enough of the language to explore Italy and get on a bus or a train, get back to the place I was staying, or walk into a market and negotiate a price in Italian, I knew that I could go anywhere in the world and be fine. This definitely gave me the courage to leave safe Ohio and move to New York City.

POUND ON!!

In my sophomore year at college, there was an audition to be the singer with the Syracuse University Big Band. The director, Steve Marcone, who is now in the music dept. at William Paterson College in NJ, told the 3 of us girls auditioning for the job to "Go find 'Shiny Stockings' and come back next week and sing it," kind of like the Wizard of Oz telling Dorothy to find the broomstick of the Wicked Witch of the West. I immediately went to a record store in downtown Syracuse, and bought a recording of Ella Fitzgerald singing 'Shiny Stockings' with The Count Basie Orchestra. I memorized it, went back the following week, and sang it for Mr. Marcone, and got the gig. The other two girls showed up, unprepared, not knowing the song, and asked me how I knew it. I said, "I went and found it!" This was a defining moment for me, proving that with hard work and smarts, I could get ahead and get the gig. It also led to 3 years of keeping the gig, and having the opportunity to sing with jazz legends Thad Jones, Mel Lewis and Phil Woods, who all visited Syracuse to do workshops with the students and perform with the big band.

After college, I had another defining moment which showed me that chutzpah and perseverance can work. There was a production of 'Fiddler on the Roof' being produced at a professional dinner theatre near my hometown. This was hands down my favorite musical since Hodel was the life story of Grandma Anna. I had always wanted to play Hodel, so the minute I heard there were auditions, I ran to the theater and auditioned with Hodel's beautifully sad song, 'Far From the Home I Love,' which I had just sung at my graduation voice recital at SU.

The director did not like me, and did not offer me the part. I was devastated, but a few days later, I went to a show at Playhouse in the Park, a renowned professional theatre in Cincinnati, and low and behold, the musical director/pianist for 'Fiddler on the Roof', Kristen Blodgett (she went on after that to work for Andrew Lloyd Weber for many years) was sitting right behind me. I overheard her say to the person she was with that she was involved with 'Fiddler', and that they had not yet cast Hodel or Tzeitel. I turned around and said, 'Excuse me, I just graduated from college with a degree in opera, I would love to audition for 'Fiddler.' She gave me the name of the producer, I called him and went for a second audition. Kristen was there at the piano, and the producer was there, but the director was not there. They both loved me, and offered me my choice of Tzeitel or Hodel. I of course took the part of Hodel.

The show, an Equity production, ran from September to December, 1979, 8 shows a week, and we received excellent reviews in all of the local papers. The harshest critic in the Cincinnati Enquirer said that I was a 'marvelous Hodel with a mesmerizing voice.' Needless to say, the director wasn't too happy with me the whole time. It turned out he was just another sleazy director that wanted to get into girls' pants, and at the audition it was probably very clear that that wasn't going to happen with me.

After Fiddler closed, Hodel and Tzeitel hopped into Hodel's Honda wagon and drove from Cincinnati to NYC. I spent 10 days in New York, and absolutely fell in love with it, and decided to move here. I had another performing job waiting for me as a singing waitress in Florida for 6 months after 'Fiddler' closed. It was my first 'dues' job. The owners of the restaurant called the job a 'college semester,' did not pay us any salary, packed the joint with 300 alta cockers from Century Village 6-nights-a-week who only tipped a nickel. We only made tips, with the carrot hanging in front of our noses that we would get $1000 if we made it to the end of the 'semester.' My friend, Equity actor from NYC Johnny Kudan, who played Perchik in Fiddler, told me I needed $3000 to move to

NYC, so I was determined to earn it.

I was the worst waitress on the planet. I did not make good tips, but I managed to get the $3000 I needed, and in August, 1980, I came to NYC to look for an apartment, and I have been here ever since. That was almost 39 years ago. When I first moved here, I was very ambitious, overly confident, somewhat naive, and pursued every little tiny lead of singing work that I could find. I immediately got hired to sing in the Trinity Church choir, on Wall Street and met jazz singer Judy Niemack there, who introduced me to the jazz scene. I got gigs in clubs right away, and started to meet lots of other singers and instrumentalists, and developed a community of peers instantly. I still sing and play with some of those wonderful musicians to this day.

My social life has always been going out to jazz clubs with my peers and friends to listen to music, and to perform it. This started way back in Cincinnati. I first heard live jazz as a 7th grader at Walnut Hills High School. We had a fantastic big band, and the minute I heard them, I was hooked on jazz for life. The director, Gary Johnston and I are now Facebook friends! There were some renowned musicians that came out of that big band, most notably pianist/composer Fred Hersch, who also moved to NYC, and has led a very productive life of recordings and compositions. He has been nominated for Grammy's countless times, and is one of the most respected pianists on the jazz scene. Marc Wolfley held down the drum chair, and has been the principal drummer with the Cincinnati Pops Orchestra since the 1980s.

In NYC, I hung out at all the clubs I could possibly go to. The 1980's were cooking with live jazz. There was a club called Bradley's on University at 11th Street, that was THE hangout for all jazz musicians, open until 4:00 a.m. If the cats weren't playing there, they would come by after their own gigs. Judy Niemack and I used to go there all the time. We saw many legends such as pianists Tommy Flannigan, Hank Jones, Michel Petrucianni and so many more, and many legendary bass players. One night, Phyllis Diller came bursting into the club, very loaded, and ran over to the piano, pushing the pianist off the bench, saying 'Lemme play the piano…." And she did! She was a good pianist. That was a fun celebrity sighting - one of many more to come!

I worked as a jazz singer regularly, and also sang at a lot of weddings, which was good money, plus whatever singing jobs I could find. I sang in several a cappella vocal groups that performed at schools, and whenever there was a vocal jazz group job, I seemed to get the call. In August of 1989, I got a phone call from John Miller, a bassist who has booked the orchestras for Broadway shows for decades. He told me that Cy Coleman had written a new show, 'City of Angels,' and that Cy wanted a vocal jazz quartet in the show ala Manhattan Transfer. I knew that this was a great call for me and I knew I was 'right' for the show. I went to the audition and aced it immediately (this was after many other auditions and gigs that I did not get.) At the audition table were Cy Coleman, playwright Larry Gelbart, musical director for the quartet Yaron Gershovsky (Manhattan Transfer's music director for more than 40 years now) and David Zippel, the lyricist.

I sang 'On The Sunny Side of the Street' and 'Moody's Mood for Love' for my audition, went out into the hall, expected to just go home, but instead was invited back into the room numerous times to sing with a combination of other singers. Finally, Cy Coleman looked at me and said, "Amy, will you be the soprano?" Thankfully, I had been in show biz long enough to know that an offer to be in a Broadway show should be answered with a resounding "Yes!"

I was out of my mind with joy! I remember heading uptown, getting off the train at Columbus Circle, calling my mom collect from a payphone and shouting, 'Mom, guess what, I'm going to be in a Broadway show!!!' My parents of course were overjoyed, and saw the show many times. I have to say, even though the show was a huge hit, nominated for 11 Tony Awards and winning 6, the best and most fun part of the entire experience was the rehearsal process. We would receive new music every day since the authors were constantly editing, so there would be daily changes. The other 3 singers in the quartet were also great readers, so we had a lot of fun reading through this very challenging music. The show was magnificent, the cast was amazing, and it was pure joy to be in the presence of such top shelf actors, Cy, Larry and David. Working with Yaron was a dream. Mom and Dad came up for opening night. My Mom bumped right into Paul Newman and Joanne Woodward after the show when she was on her way up to my dressing room. I bumped into Angela Lansbury back stage, who told me I was 'Marvelous!' My reply was, of course, 'YOU'RE marvelous!' Bill and Hillary were at opening night, and there was a constant stream of celebs and luminaries coming by to see the show.

It was a grand time in my life, and a huge feather in my cap. I felt so very lucky to have that job, but I also felt that I won it and that I deserved it.

When I first moved to NYC, even though I had performing work right away, it wasn't enough to cover my expenses, so considering what a sucky waitress I was, I got a job as a prep cook in a restaurant, including working for Suzanne Levine, owner of the famous Sarabeth's. (I was a migrant fruit cutter. I used to spend days prepping the fruit for those adorable Ball jars of jam that she still sells.) I have to say, I learned so much watching her work so hard and grow that business, she is so successful, and was a great role model. I had several of these types of jobs for the first 4 years I lived in NYC. At the time, they paid $5 an hour under the table, and I could eat on the job as well as take food home, so I had very low grocery bills, and combined with my music work, I got by.

One day in 1984, Judy Niemack said to me, "Amy, why don't you teach?" I had never thought about being a voice teacher, but I thought it was a good idea, so I went down to the New School, and got a job teaching at The Guitar Study Center, a rock and roll school lodged at the New School, founded by Eddie

Simon, Paul's brother. Around that time, I was at a jam session at The Angry Squire, a club that used to be on Seventh Avenue and 22 Street. The pianist invited me to sit in, I called a tune, the key, counted it in and off I went. It was fine, everybody liked it. Then, another singer got up to sing. She called the tune, and the pianist said,'What key?" and she giggled and said "I dunno,' so the pianist rolled his eyes and shouted to the bass player, "Eb." Then he said, can you count us in, and she giggled and said 'I dunno....' so he counted her in, 1, 2, 1234.

This was a pivotal moment for me. My mouth dropped open, I couldn't believe my eyes, that a singer would get up on a stage in NYC and not know what she was doing, instilling the wrath of the band who had to now babysit her. This is what I call, "The Chick Singer Mentality." It's the old stereotype of the girl singer not knowing what to do, behaving unprofessionally, and having to lean on the band to do her job as well as theirs, resulting in the disdain and disrespect of the band. This leads them to the opinion that singers don't know shit, and perpetuates the myth of the woman as a sex object - just a pretty girl propped up on the bandstand to look good fronting the band.

At that moment, my future life was instantly defined. I set out on a path as a vocal jazz educator to teach singers to 'know their shit,' as we say in the jazz world and this is how I have made my living my entire life since that moment. I have been an adjunct professor at The New School for Jazz and Contemporary Music since then; I am in my 33rd year there. I have been adjunct professor at City College Jazz for 6 years, and I created the vocal department at the enormously successful after school program for teens, Jazz House Kids, in Montclair, NJ, which is run by dynamo woman Melissa Walker, and her husband Christian McBride, one of the most successful bassists in the world. Christian has won 6 Grammys for his own recordings as a leader, is on hundreds of other records as a side man, is on Sirius radio, NPR Live From Lincoln Center Jazz and directs both the Newport Jazz Festival and NJPAC jazz series.

Throughout my teaching career of 36 years, I have taught hundreds of singers, predominantly young women, to be well prepared and educated jazz singing professionals, ready to be equal players on the band stand, and to earn their reputations on their merits, and not have to be propped up by the band. Thus the title,

'Dispelling the Myth of the Chick Singer.' I have devoted my entire teaching career to it.

Over the span of nearly 39 years on the jazz scene in NYC, I have performed and recorded a fair amount. I have 5 recordings as a leader, and I am singing on many other records as a 'sidewoman.' I have performed on Broadway, traveled the world to sing at jazz clubs in Russia, Turkey, Greece, England, Italy, France, Belgium, Brazil, Puerto Rico, Canada, more, and all around the US. Not only am I a world renowned jazz educator, but I have led summer jazz camps and workshops globally for 15 years. I have sung on several film scores and TV commercials, and on several educational books and DVDs.

Perhaps the recording I am most proud of is The Royal Bopsters Project, my 3rd recording on the Motema record label. This was a 5 year project, from start to finish, released in 2015, the idea for which I came up with - singing in a vocal quartet alongside some of our greatest living bebop singing heroes. The recording features 5 vocal jazz legends: Mark Murphy, Jon Hendricks and Bob Dorough, now departed and sorely missed, and the female jazz singing heroines Annie Ross and Sheila Jordan. I sing soprano in the quartet along with my pals Holli Ross, alto, Pete McGuinness, tenor and Dylan Pramuk, bass. This project was my idea; I was the creative director and executive producer of it, and it made a big splash on the jazz scene.

We have released our second recording, and performed at the Newport Jazz Festival, in August 2019. We performed in Athens, Greece and in London, England. I am also proud of my solo singing CD, 'Bridges', which represents my recordings form the late 1980s and early 1990s, with a stellar cast of jazz musicians, Both of these recordings still receive regular airplay on WBGO, years after their releases. WBGO is the largest jazz radio station in the world, and a very important component of the jazz scene here in NYC.

In conjunction with my nearly 39-year career in NYC, I have raised two amazing, independent and socially conscious daughters, Sofia and Anna, both in their 20s. My children grew up hearing the best music; a combination of the greatest jazz singers such as Ella Fitzgerald, Billie Holiday, Mark Murphy, Joe Williams, Teri Thornton, Lambert, Hendricks and Ross, as well as the great Broadway cast recordings featuring such legends as Ethel Merman,

Judy Garland, Julie Andrews, Fred Astaire, Bonnie's father John Raitt and Jerry Orbach. My girls were both born in NYC. We were living in a medium-sized apartment, but when it came time to be a school chaser, and I learned that my two-year-old daughter would have to be tested to go to nursery school, I decided to take the suburban plunge to avoid the madness that is getting your child into the 'right' schools in NYC. I looked for houses in the 'suburban ring' for about a year - Westchester, Bergen County, Essex County. I focused on some of the more arty fartsy areas, such as Ossining, Dobbs Ferry, Hastings in Westchester, and Montclair, Maplewood, Engelwood and Teaneck in NJ. I settled on Teaneck, not only for its proximity to NYC and ease of driving into town, but because Teaneck was the first public school system in the US to voluntarily integrate. Teaneck has a history of African American jazz musicians moving there to raise their families in a friendly, accepting community of lovely homes and a good school system, so we moved to Teaneck when the girls were very small. They went to Teaneck public schools for nearly all of Elementary, Middle and High school. Their circle of friends included kids of every color, religion and sexual orientation, which is what I envisioned for them. I did look at houses in lily white suburban areas and made the decision that I did not want my kids raised in that world. As a result, they are both very well adjusted to the world, and still have friends of all stripes. This was my dream for them, more important to me than their grades, or their achievements in their careers. The most important thing in life is to be able to get along with people, all people, and to not segregate oneself in some insular community. My children live successfully in the world, are compassionate, smart, open minded, artistic and funny. I could not be more proud of both of them.

In conclusion, and to reflect on some of the choices I have made in my life, what I have accomplished, and who my greatest role models are, I will start with my parents. Though I rejected my parents' insular Jewish community that was very segregated and one dimensional, they were both hard workers and ethical people, and I inherited a great work ethic from both of them. My Dad in particular, although emotionally distant, was a self-starter, very creative and smart, and worked very, very hard and diligently. He took care of our family in the only way he knew how. He brought home the 'corned beef,' (instead of bacon, we were semi-Kosher!)

and was very committed to my mother and to us, in spite of the fact that he had no idea how to talk to us. My mom was warm, funny, smart and extraordinarily kind and generous. She was very popular and highly trusted amongst her large community in Cincinnati, so well respected and loved in our extended family, and had a way of making strangers feel instantly welcomed. I credit my Mom with unknowingly giving me the ability to walk into a room of strangers and immediately make friends and feel at ease. She took great care of us, and taught me how to be a good mom and take care of my family. She also schlepped me to 5 million piano, voice, dance and drama lessons, skills which I use in my adult life on a daily basis.

I knew from the age of 12 that I wanted to be a professional singer. Once I heard Laura Nyro's records, and saw the big band at school, my path was set for life. I consider myself very lucky to have achieved this on several counts: my parents had enough money to finance my education, and support me in my endeavors. They were absolutely supportive of my performing career, and were always thrilled with my accomplishments. I know that this is not the case for lots of people, and I am extremely grateful for the unconditional love and support I received from my parents.

I am very grateful to have been able to spend my entire life in the world of jazz and on the stage. I have worked hard for this, and I feel that I have earned what I have been rewarded with. I have had to tolerate a lot of bullshit and rejection, both professional and personal, I still do - it is ever present. I did not deal with rejection well at all when I first started out, I have learned to develop a very thick skin about it, and also recognize that there are always more opportunities out there. You just have to find them, or create them.

You have to be willing to hang in there and do whatever it takes to get what you want. It is very important to me that my goals have not involved hurting anyone. I feel proud that I have managed to be successful without leaving any dead bodies on the side of the road. Also, perhaps the experience of feeling a little bit like an outsider, never feeling like I was one of the 'pretty girls' who just had things handed to them because they looked good, was actually a positive experience for me. It forced me to look outside the box and find my own path, maybe around the obstacles, instead of confronting them, but still leading to my goals.

POUND ON!!

My advice for young women: stay the course. Keep in mind exactly what it is you want, while constantly re-examining yourself and being open to changes here and there. Be ethical. Don't kill other people to get what you want, because at the end of the day, you have to look in the mirror and be ok with yourself. Be willing to accept defeat when it comes, give yourself a little break to recuperate and re-energize, and get back on the horse.

NEVER believe someone when they tell you if you sleep with them you will get jobs x, y and z. It never works out, ever, usually it backfires, because word gets around. You have to earn your own credentials, and base your reputation and your work on your skills and knowledge, not your looks and sex appeal.

Lastly, follow your instincts and don't second guess yourself. You can second guess yourself into complete disaster and depression. Your instincts are usually right. Follow them, stand by them and work hard to complete what needs to be done. NEVER let anyone tell you you're not good enough, or you can't do this or that. If people treat you that way, they are trying to manipulate you and stop you from achieving, because they are weak and jealous.

We always have the power to do what we want, even if it takes an unusual path to get there. Stick to your guns, and believe in yourself, because if you don't believe in yourself, nobody else will.

POUND ON!!

COMMON THEMES

We are Very Different but Have A Lot in Common...

All of my Alphas are extremely successful, impressive women. I enjoyed all of our discussions and looked so forward to our talks and interviews. Each was incredibly open, reflective and generous in sharing her experiences and I was truly awed by the grit, determination and perseverance I heard in their stories. I have known some of my Alphas for decades, but didn't know their whole story, what motivated them, who influenced them, and why they ended up where they are now. Every Alpha told me they found this reflective exercise to be very cathartic. They had never taken the time to understand themselves in this way, or to deeply examine where they came from and where they derived their power. They also immensely enjoyed the trip down memory lane, conjuring up long-lost relatives and memories, and reliving the safe, earlier times in their lives. Their memories and mine were not always pleasant or positive, and their tenacity in "pounding on" surprised them. They would tell me in our talks that they couldn't believe how much they had done, and how much they had been through. Step by step we advanced through adversity and change, often without stopping long enough to savor the moment. There simply wasn't time, and there was too much to do. We have all learned at some level to stop and smell the roses, but it's really not our nature.

We all came from different places with different experiences, but as I chatted with each Alpha I started to see and hear some common themes emerge. No matter how different our paths, we shared some commonalities which I now proudly and humbly share with you.

1. Hard work really does pay off

It should really go without saying, but I'll say it anyway: hard work really does pay off. All my Alphas are amazingly hard workers. We have defined goals and tasks, and high expectations of what we need to accomplish every day. Every day is a precious gift and experience, and no Alpha wants to waste it or not meet her goals.

Every Alpha chose a profession where success is impossible without hard work. Several became lawyers which requires years of study, countless hours of reading, exams and qualifying programs which are rigorous to say the least. We have Alphas who built their own businesses from scratch, who dared many years ago to take the risk of walking away from secure jobs and high salaries to venture out on their own. Being self-employed sounds empowering and glamorous, but takes days, weeks, months and years of hard work to succeed. Our Alphas did it with families and many other responsibilities. Those of us who held demanding jobs in large companies devoted thousands of woman hours to the betterment of those entities, often toiling away at great personal expense. We each had our own reasons to find the drive and passion to work this way, but work this way we did. Great success, even positive, attainable success, takes hard work, and lots of it.

2. We were born lucky

All Alphas featured in this book were born lucky. We didn't have to fight to survive as young children. We were all born into families where we were loved, cherished, and cared for, mostly by close relatives. Our families were by no means perfect, and some dysfunction would require therapy to fix (like my father wanting a boy), but we had secure homes and relatively secure family relationships as small children. All of us had well-furnished homes, running water and food on the table. Worries about the basics of survival were not our collective experience. Those types of struggles were endured by the generations before us, many of whom emigrated from far-away places and came to North America with very little. With the exception of Irene who was born in Taiwan, we were born in either Canada or the United States, as were most of our parents and some of our grandparents.

It is abundantly clear that our early nurturing environments allowed us to grow and thrive without concern for our own survival. Our environments allowed us the freedom to focus on higher level needs like relationships in our families, celebrations, social relationships, sports and fun activities, and then the privilege of going to school. It's not like we had to worry about having money for groceries - our devoted families took care of those worries for us. It was only later and upon reflection that we can see how very lucky we were to have had families who took such good care of us.

I was once part of a panel at work where we were speaking to high school students about our backgrounds. A European colleague of mine made a comment about having a very "privileged" childhood because she had running water and food on the table every night. One of the American students told me afterward she'd expected my colleague to say that "she was a princess or something", when she said she was privileged. The girl had never thought about her good fortune in growing up in a middle-class family in the secure NJ suburbs. We Alphas probably never thought too much about it either. We were born lucky into families with means in a society where girls are permitted to go to school. Our strong families gave us a very strong start.

Along with providing us with basic sustenance and emotional support, we also got a lot of encouragement from our families for the things we wanted to do in life. While there was some independence and rebellion, like Lynda moving away, and me going to a school my family disapproved of, there was also a lot of family pride in our achievements and help along the way. My father told me he would help me, Amy 's parents encourage her musical and show biz aspirations, Sally's father employed her to help grow his business, and the list goes on. While we may not have always followed their advice, knowing that they were behind us early on made it much easier for us to follow our dreams.

3. Strong Family Values

Along with being born lucky in terms of the basics and then some, and having supportive encouraging parents, we Alphas also came from families with strong values and integrity. (Except maybe some of Cheryl Goldhart's interesting extended family!).

It took many of us a while in the workplace, and the experience of getting knocked down a few times, to understand that others don't have our integrity or share the values we were taught. Lee talks a lot about honesty. Lynda talks about office politics and sabotage by those who wanted her to fail. "Watch your back" she says in her story. No doubt a hard-fought lesson after growing up in families that would not have prepared us for such back-stabbing and ambushes.

4. Gratitude for the strong, loving women who came before us

We all know that role models set the stage for us and form our view of how to approach the world and our lives in general. Role models are everywhere - both good and bad - and are often seen in pop culture, movies, on tv and in music videos. They do not necessarily provide good values or models to live by, but they are most certainly everywhere we look. If we are smart, we can ignore the bad role models, or take them for what is a side effect of our modern-day technologies, Internet and information flows.

Technology has changed current role models with the advent of social media. Those channels provide platforms for all manner of influence and influencers, and have allowed some very odd, seedy characters to become wealthy as supporters of esoteric fashion and lifestyle brands. My Grandma Jeannie would be horrified. She was once handed a magazine on the Toronto waterfront. "I've never seen such filth in all my life!" she exclaimed. I often wonder what she would think of the things we now accept as the norm in pop culture.

We Alphas, on the other hand, all had very strong female influences and role models growing up. Our mothers and grandmothers took care of us and our families even if men abandoned them as they did in Lee's family. Lynda's family had a breadwinner "disappear" too. This left our ancestral women with great responsibility at a time when it was virtually impossible for a women to get a decent job, let alone earn a good living and support a family. Amy's grandmother came from persecution and poverty in Russia and chose domestic servitude in Cincinnati, Ohio over a sweatshop job in NYC. Some choice. No wonder she was so happy to be married, have a family, and be able to cook and care for her children and grandchildren. We can hardly imagine an experience like hers, or the women who were abandoned. How did they survive and end up so loving and dedicated to us? We are all very grateful.

We Alphas had the luxury of some economic stability as well as the benefit of living with and being loved by extraordinary "ordinary" women. They taught us perseverance and independence, resourcefulness, and how to love. They also left an indelible mark on how we face life's challenges. Incredibly, we Alphas have all modeled our lives to honor them in some way; whether it's through following their lessons or emulating their values, our hard work and tenacity honors them every day. We are all keenly aware of what they did for us, and of the legacy they left behind. We all feel the need to pay it forward. It is also very clear that we all still feel their loss and think them often and with gratitude. Our attainable careers would have made them proud, and we all wish we could have shared more time with them. I often say I would give everything I own for one more day with my mother. I mean it.

Regardless of their lack of physical presence today, our strong ancestral Alpha women live on in our hearts and in the lessons we teach our own daughters. We all benefit from the perseverance and love of the early Alpha women who helped shape our lives.

All my Alphas try to be good role models. We feel an enormous responsibility to the women coming up behind us to leave our world and companies better places than we found them. By being good role models we not only honor our ancestral matriarchs, we continue the legacy of their work.

5. The Mean Girls and other bullies

To my great surprise I found during the Alpha interviews that many of us had negative social experiences for a variety of reasons in many settings. All my Alphas are very well-adjusted adults with large networks of friends, colleagues and acquaintances. However, each of us learned something about early social rejection and feeling excluded from "cool" or accepted groups throughout our developmental years.

Socialization and feeling part of a broader social order is a fundamental, basic human need. It is third on the Maslow hierarchy of needs after physiology and safety, and is termed "love and belonging". Animals ostracized or lost from their packs can't survive in the wild. Similarly, in the jungle of schools and workplaces, being ignored, sidelined or excluded can have devastating and long-lasting psychological impacts. Clicks of girls who are "in" and girls who are "out" start early in childhood. Girls with valued traits are generally the ringleaders - those with good looks, some kind of special talent, or simply the ability to attract and influence others. It's the attraction that is often so mysterious. What is it about the leaders of the "cool crowd" that allows them to attract others to follow them blindly into the river like the Pied Piper? To an outsider, the attraction is not understood, but is very visibly observed. It's like John Travolta's character in the movie Grease - the coolest, albeit simple-minded, bad boy in the town from the proverbial wrong side of the tracks, who gets the cutest, incredibly beautiful painfully skinny and perfect wealthy girl. I always thought that there was an inverse relationship between the coolest kids and basic human intelligence; intelligence dropped as coolness increased. The cool kids were street smart, kind of like pack animals, but seemed not to have much intellect. Maybe that was just my "sour grapes" coming through after being excluded and bullied. "If you don't want us, that's fine -- you're not smart enough for us anyway." Looking back, I think the mean girls were probably even more insecure than I was. They just covered it up with lipstick, trendy clothes and bravado.

In talking with my Alphas, I found that many of us were socially excluded, especially in our teen years. If we were good at school, the books and attendant success were our friends. The kids of the in crowd generally didn't do that well in school, and spent more time socializing as an outlet for acceptance and gratification.

Social success was their validation. Except for Lee, who had lots of friends, the rest of us found our validation and salvation in our book reports, high marks and good test scores. School was our friend, she accepted us. Every day, no matter how we were treated socially, school welcomed us with open arms, reinforced our intellectual capability, and was there for us through thick and thin with objective approval.

The mean girls, however, were everywhere in high school, and followed us into the workplace as well. I experienced the mean girls first at summer camp as a 10-year-old. Lynda was surrounded by them in Thunder Bay, Ontario growing up where they even tricked her into thinking they had a "playdate" organized. It doesn't end with childhood. As a young adult, a few of the mean girls from camp tried to lose me en route to one of their houses and then wouldn't answer the doorbell when I got there. All these years later these events form indelible bad memories. They were early lessons in rejection and exclusion which leave profound scars in the ability to trust and form strong bonds of friendship. You just never knew what you were going to get (or not get). We learn to move past them once we find like-minded people and have positive social experiences, but it's a tough start.

Exclusion can be mean in other ways as well. Take Amy, who is beautiful and immensely talented, but not "Twiggy" as she describes herself. Being in show business and coping with this kind of meanness and rejection could have crippled her. Instead, she educated herself, turned to school, and made herself better informed, skilled and capable than the skinny giggly "accepted girls". Way to Pound On!!, but those feelings of exclusion have stuck with her all these years after too, and could have had lasting negative effects on her self-confidence and self-esteem.

The mean girls and other exclusion affected us Alphas deeply. Mean girl treatment shaped our view of social relationships and where we fit in to the order of things, whether at camp, school, show business or the workplace. These experiences taught us what it feels like to be left out, and that we should, rather, include people and treat them with kindness so that no one would feel like we did, at least not if we can help it.

I understand now how profoundly the nasty mean girls and other bullies affected us. In a sense, though, they did us all a favor.

Without their "approval and acceptance" we had to find success and validation (i.e. love and belonging) in other ways. We learned to cope in difficult situations that the mean girls wouldn't potentially confront for decades. Their early social success was in some ways to their detriment. It caused many to compromise their educations or plans for the future. They chose the in crowd over school and future career planning because it wasn't cool to do well in school. In those pre-teen and teenaged moments, your friends and social click are everything. With maturity, we learn that they are not. There are many more important things in life like good health, loving spouses, and happy children.

Social success and acceptance in high school or college is no predictor of any kind of success later on. Workplaces are also fraught with other kinds of "mean girls" and unkind people (we'll get to that when we talk about women mentors) many of whom don't succeed or aren't happy either. We Alphas were more prepared than others to deal with these people given our early social experiences. In the end, the mean girls were just a blip on our radar screen as we've ascended through our lives and left them behind. We should recognize what we learned from these lessons and Pound On!!

6. The Three R's Mattered - Getting a good education was important to us and to our families

All of my Alphas have extremely impressive academic credentials, most of us with several university degrees and accreditations. Education is the gateway and foundation to opportunity in our society. Educational success is highly valued in most families, and academic success is celebrated and rewarded. Get an "A" and you'll get a prize, we would often hear. Reading, writing and 'rithmetic set us up to get good jobs later in life. Our parents, notably our mothers, got us off to school every morning with the tools for success - lunch or lunch money, books and supplies, breakfast and completed homework and supplies. And they were (or many of them were) there when we got home, or sent us to capable babysitters. We got help with our homework, projects, assignments and presentations. They also carted us around to our extra-curricular activities which formed part of and enhanced our educations. My mother took us to all our music and dance lessons, sports and activities. Amy's mother, who had two other daughters, took her to all manner of voice and music lessons. Lynda learned piano and to ski outside of school where she always had her nose in a book or novel of some kind -- even hidden in her math book in class. Clearly our parents and grandparents saw the value of education of all kinds both inside and outside the traditional classroom. They encouraged and supported us, as well as invested time and money in our development and enjoyment of school and other interests.

School and education is a ticket out; out of poverty, out of mundane jobs and careers, out of small towns we want to escape, and big cities we felt lost in. Lynda came to the big city to go to school, as Amy did to pursue her Broadway dreams. I fled the big city for a smaller venue where I thought I'd fit in better and could leave behind the painful loss of my mother.

Interestingly, many of my Alphas were the first in their families to go to University. Cheryl was working in her mother's jewelry and antique store when an insult ("Go wash my Rolls") by a wealthy client catapulted her back to finish high school. Lynda's family members had educations, especially the women, but not at the high level of hers. Similarly, Lee's parents did not have the means to pursue higher education opportunities.

The common thread and theme, however, is that we all knew a great education would afford us independence and self-determination. With a job and our own money, we would be independent and could make our own decisions. Education provided us that gateway, and we were determined to get in. How and where we got our educations varies. Some of us stayed close to home while others ventured far away. Early work experiences, like Lynda's bad moments in law, drove her back to school to re-examine her choices. Cheryl had a similar unhappy experience and went back to school to study psychology. My first career in teaching wasn't satisfying enough for me, so I went to law school. Lee continued her education for many years so she could better help her consulting clients after she bravely formed her own consulting business. All interesting choices but with one strong commonality - when we wanted to change our lives and upgrade our positions, we went back to school.

We all worked very hard for our educations and professional designations and training. They took years to complete, but allowed us immeasurable career opportunities and choices. Our paper chase gave us our fine start to climbing the walls.

7. Our Women Mentors at work - or lack of them

In addition to having a lack of professional women mentors in school, and very little social acceptance by girls in our early experiences, our workplaces did little to provide women mentors either.

When we Alphas were in professional schools, the proportion of women in those programs was very low. Our first workplaces (and some now) were no different. There were very few women outside of the administrative staff and very few role models or potential mentors. Lee talks about having great mentors and sponsors, but they were men. Sally had her father as her first boss and mentor. The rest of us describe a somewhat different experience.

Those of us who started in professional firms found very few women there. If there were women in the firm, they made it very clear that they had no interest in helping any of us. We never expected the men to help us, but the women not helping us was a disappointing surprise. Mentoring and its benefits were not really widely understood in those days. Engagement of young talent was not seen as the task of employers or more senior professionals.

We were told we were lucky to have jobs, and we honestly believed that, at least at first. Not wanting to rock the boat led us to put up with a lot of crap and lousy treatment. Without the support and protection of the women who were there before us, we were left to fend for ourselves with the unruly men in their boys' clubs. The more senior women felt no obligation or desire to help us, and they said so. They thought that since they had paid their dues, that we should too. We see this theme in my story, Lynda's, Cheryl 's, and in a different way in Amy's show biz story. This blatant lack of care for women coming up behind us still persists in some environments with some women. I once had a very senior European woman tell me - "While I'm here in the US I don't intend to do anything for the women here, so don't ask me". Another woman more recently honored for professional accomplishments admonished those who wanted to congratulate her for being the first woman to win a prestigious award. She didn't think gender had anything to do with it, which was really not the case or the real message. The first woman to win a prestigious STEM award should be celebrated as an example and role model for the next generation. Not wanting to be a role model in that circumstance does not help the women who are currently making career choices. Denying it cheats everyone and undermines progress.

The behavior of the senior women we encountered was very exclusionary and discouraging. These days, diversity and inclusion is well-recognized as essential to business success. Customers need to have confidence that their suppliers operate with integrity and respect, and many require certain diversity standards or they won't do business with you. The behavior of women at the top not wanting to help us flies in the face of these objectives. We never felt included in the culture of the places we worked at the beginning of our careers, which truly hurt everyone. We looked up and saw very few people like us, or people we wanted to be like. This led all of us in different directions. I went in-house to a big corporation, Cheryl opened her own law firm, Lynda left and worked in other environments and opened her own firm. Our decisions might have been different had we been included, and had our female "role models" stepped in and stepped up. It cost them - firms and companies make big investments in training when they bring in employees who are early in career. When we leave after a few years we take everything we learned with us, and rightfully so. Mentoring keeps good people. Feeling included does too. Not having good senior female role models hurt everyone, and is a common refrain in our stories.

8. Gender Discrimination and Sexual Harassment

The purpose of this book is to tell positive stories of success for us Alphas. Many of us had early loss, struggles and problems along the way, but we persevered, worked hard, used what we had, and achieved. We are voracious students of our chosen fields, and have the desire to help others in meaningful ways. Since this book and our stories are meant to be a positive chronicle (albeit truthful, and not all recounts are blissful) to inspire and help give other women the courage to pursue their dreams, I don't want to focus too much on gender discrimination and sexual harassment as part of our stories. I have a later section of the book that talks about concepts, which outlines the impact and presence of gender discrimination in the workplace, pay inequity, and some other issues women face at work because of gender. There are many, and there is still much work to be done. However, for this topic, in this work, suffice it to say that all Alphas have experienced various forms of gender discrimination whether in sabotage, lack of opportunity, getting less interesting work, or having to overcome a "chick singer" mentality. We rose above all of it, found our voices, or voted with our feet if it got unbearable.

I would like us to focus more on how we deal with such topics, rather than on the incidents or events themselves. Let's look at how we coped, what we learned, and how we can continue to effect change. With this focus we recognize these problems and tackle them with our eyes wide open. Together, we blaze the trail so that those coming up behind us can more easily walk through the jungle, and metaphorically climb the walls. We thereby pull them up to join us in pounding on the glass ceiling.

Most importantly we need to raise our voices and speak up for ourselves and other women. Silence perpetuates the problems of discrimination and harassment and shames the victims. We should encourage women to come forward if there are issues, support each other through a journey of healing, and hold perpetrators accountable for their words and deeds.

9. We accomplish nothing alone -- it takes a village

We've heard it over and over again, especially when it comes to raising children: it takes a village. Whether we came from families with means or not, there were hundreds of people and extensive resources involved in raising us. Our extended families -- parents, grandparents, aunts, uncles, cousins and siblings were there from the beginning, shaping us, caring for us, and giving us guidance and guideposts along the way. Then came a broader more extended world of educators, both secular and non-secular. We all went to school, most of us had religious training, and those fortunate enough had activities, lessons, camps and groups we joined. All of these groups, lessons, teachers, artists, athletes, artisans and role models were part of our village. We remember our early teachers, and what a strong influence they had on us. Amy, Lynda and I had a myriad of instructors for all of our activities and lessons. Many of us had "villages" which included getting back to nature. Summer camps are full of peer and teenaged teachers who mentored and guided some of us in skills of privilege like boating and horse back riding. Lynda skied with friends and had a family camp up north. I went to summer camps and a Toronto boating club.

This exposure and its benefits took a true army of many dedicated people year after year. Some were relatives, some volunteers, others paid instructors, but what they taught us is woven into the fabric of our childhoods and teenaged years, through and into college and university programs. All the people who taught us and exposed us to these great experiences were part of our villages, and it didn't stop there.

Our careers have taken a village to build, construct and maintain too. Our towns, camps, cottages, neighborhoods and schools all converged into our workplaces where we found another "village". There were many people along the way we learned from, lessons both good and bad, but influences nonetheless. Our projects and assignments were mostly done in teams. We started out as individual contributors working alone, but this changed as time went on. When the work got more complex and we ascended and got more experience, we needed teams of people to help drive success. We learned, some of us the hard way, that we don't do anything alone. To accomplish anything we needed to inspire, motivate, drive, supervise and sometimes even discipline our teams. It took that whole village to get us where we are, and it takes our continuing village of networks to sustain us here as well. We've built relationships in our professional villages and leveraged them to enhance our careers. This also takes strategic input, drive and opportunity, often provided by other Alphas.

The town "villages" remained important to us even once we entered the workforce. We have children and parents. We've all had a spouse, some of us more than one. We've needed villages to balance and juggle our careers and families along our journeys. If we've had the means we've had nannies and housekeepers. Many of us have at least needed babysitters and afterschool programs. Our children had activities which required organization and transportation. Our parents have their own villages for support as well, like Lee's 103-year-old (amazing) mother. I've often reflected on how all the people who help me in my life required payment of some kind. Even the woman who walks my dog. Our careers allow us to hire resources to take care of everyone, but it still takes a village to do it.

All these "villages" from early childhood to our career networks, our children's and parents' villages have all gotten us to where we are now. We are very grateful for them all.

10. Give back and forward - to others and to ourselves

We Alphas know that we were all born lucky. Whether we came from families with wealth, or middle class means, we know we started a step ahead and with many advantages others don't have. We know these advantages in love, care and education formed us and allowed us to become Alphas. Without these advantages we might have gotten here, but it would have been much less likely and a lot harder.

All of us talk about giving back. We give back to earlier in career women, our families, friends, network and peers. We have strong consciences which make sure we help others as part of our life's mission. Lee jumped in with ideas as soon as I told her about this project. Cheryl has helped me immeasurably with personal legal matters. I like to think I helped her through tough times as well. Lynda saved me from the trials and tribulations we encountered as early lawyers by sharing the journey with me. Sally helped me establish a network when I moved to the US and started a new job. I reconnected with Amy, a childhood friend, when I moved to NJ. She reconnected me to our childhoods.

We have helped and guided each other through careers,

marriages, divorces, children and many other life events. I hope I've given back as well. When I told Lee about this book, she said, "All the good karma you've put into the world will come back to you now." I must have given some, because I've already gotten back 1000 fold more than I ever thought I gave.

All of us understand that we need to pay forward as well as back. We work on paving the way for the next generation, and try to live in ways that keep the planet sustained. We are all involved in mentoring and teaching. We sit on boards and participate in our communities. We find time to spend with those who ask and those in need. I am awed by the work of my Alphas, and how they make time for everyone and everything. I hope they make time for themselves.

Paying it back and forward is not just for others, our communities and our planet. It is for each and every one of us all. We need to care for ourselves and nurture our needs and desires, or we won't be able to care for anyone or anything else. This important lesson usually comes to us late. It is in our nature to nurture and care for others, but not really to care for ourselves. How many times do we say "I'll go to the gym tomorrow, or next week"....or "I'll take a vacation soon and try to unplug"...which always turns out to be an impossibility. We need to pay back, pay forward, and pay ourselves too. If we don't take care of ourselves we won't be able to take charge or take care of anyone else.

ALPHA(S) RULE(S)

Make your own life decisions even if others disagree.

Speak up for yourself and others.

Live your life balance.

Take on meaningful work, whatever that means to you.

Earn your own money (i.e. learn to type so you won't starve).

Find your voice early and use it often.

Help other women whenever you can, especially women who are early in their career who can learn from your example.

Self-evaluate every day and try to do better every tomorrow.

Remember that failure shouldn't be an option. Learn from it if it is.

Be proud of how you behave.

If it doesn't feel right, don't do it.

Be true to yourself.

Show empathy, not softness.

Remember that others are not like you and accept it.

Don't try to fix other people or their problems.

Share and seek personal information wisely and sparingly.

Don't say anything behind people's backs that you wouldn't say to their face – especially your boss.

POUND ON!!

Pretend your boss is looking over your shoulder before you hit “send”.

Be fair, just and honest.

Embrace change and new challenges.

Get the question right.

Feel the room and react.

Demand and give respect.

Don’t get pushed around.

Give back with gratitude.

Make your own rules.

POUND ON!!

HOW TO CLIMB THE WALLS

Barriers, Obstacles and (the rare) Helping Hands: What the research shows about gender norms in the workplace and how to overcome them

This chapter is meant as an overview of concepts which appear in the research literature around gender and leadership. I've touched on the various concepts in my Alpha stories. This information is a high level introduction to give you a vocabulary for discussion of the issues women face in the workforce. Take it as part of the instruction guide to ensure that we all feel supported on our climb, understand the reasons for our challenges, and find the helping hands we need to give and receive along the way.

It is clear from the research that women and men experience the workplace quite differently, and are viewed very differently within it. Without the helping hands of other women, we have largely been left on our own to navigate through the maze of gender norms and unwritten rules ourselves. Sadly for us Alphas, we would have fared much better with any support from other women, both leaders and peers alike. Our stories all indicate very little female support on our climbs. Even a very recent study by the University of Notre Dame and Northwestern University revealed that women with a solid support group of other women are more likely to attain high-ranking leadership positions[1]. Our ascents were all made much more difficult because we were unknowingly threatening the existing male-dominated power structure. Also without knowing it, we were walking a tightrope. Read on.

The Double-Bind: Walking the Tightrope

Women leaders face the need to be seen as warm and nice, as well as competent and tough at the same time[2]. Researchers say that this creates a "double bind" or a "catch-22" for women leaders who are either seen as "bimbos" or "bitches". I would take this even further and say we really have a triple bind. To say we have to be nice and warm or strong and tough is only part of the equation. The third part, or the triplet part of the bind is being underestimated or assumed incompetent for the task or job in the first place. To say we struggle with deciding on appearing too nice or too strong overlooks the fundamental issue of whether we are seen to even have a right to be in the job. We need to prove that we are worthy of the job in the first place. Think about our Alpha stories. I was continually underestimated as an early in career lawyer as either being too young, too inexperienced or lacking the capability to do the job, and was repeatedly told so by clients and lawyers alike. Amy had to overcome the "chick singer" stereotypes through education and capability. Both Cheryl and Lynda had such poor early validation as lawyers that they questioned whether law was the right career for them and took different paths for a while. This is a disappointing reflection after spending years training for entry into the profession. Never underestimate the impact of underestimating someone else. It hurts, and hurts our confidence, but in the end it made us Alphas even more determined to prove ourselves. I'm not sure why we had the tenacity to persevere, but we did. Again, the third arm of the triple bind is being underestimated and/or perceived as unworthy of being in the position. Too nice or too tough only matters if people think you should be there in the first place.

Emily Bazelon interviewed Katherine Phillips of Columbia University and Shelley Correll of Stanford for a recent article in the New York Times Magazine[3]. Bazelon also talks about the "double bind" as the distinction between taking care and taking charge. She examines the impact of the "bind" on salary negotiations, and in particular, indicates that women settle for lower salaries than men when negotiating. Furthermore, those women who negotiate for high salaries are not positively viewed upon entry into the jobs[3]. This fits with my additional third point or "triple bind" - being underestimated and assumed unworthy of the job in the first place. With little validation or encouragement, we are our own worst enemies on the ascent. Women didn't help us, and we were severely underestimated by others, as well as by ourselves.

Zheng, et al. talk about the "demanding yet caring" contrast as the first of four paradoxes, or as part of a balancing act. The need to be demanding yet caring is the first paradox. Our feedback may not be positive after driving hard, and we question whether a man would have gotten the same comments. Who knows, but I submit that it is highly unlikely. The second paradox centers on the need to be authoritative yet participative at the same time.[2]

In a similar vein to the first paradox, women in the study felt a strong need to be collaborative at the same time as being confident and assertive. Paradox three is not much more encouraging -- the need to advocate for ourselves while serving others. Are we waitresses seeking a higher wage? And the fourth is equally difficult -- to maintain a distance while still being approachable. How is that really possible, I ask myself? We start sounding like superwomen -- which ordinary woman could possibly navigate all these contradictions and paradoxes?[2]

How can we be distant and approachable, an authority figure and a participant, serve as well as advocate and care for others while we take charge? And all of this while questioning whether we should be in the job in the first place, which is the third or triplet piece of the bind. It's enough to make you want to strangle yourself on the rope of impossibility. Zheng, et al, do have some strategies to manage this myriad of demands, which I'll refer to and comment on next.[2]

Zheng sets out some practical advice, like adapt to the situation, by not always sitting at the head of the table, for example. Try to be nice first and then tough, i.e. build relationships and establish trust before getting too directive. Look for wins, focus on the tasks, and try to reinforce the positive. All good advice, but I sum it all up as saying "be human". We are Alphas, true, but we are not Super Woman, Wonder Woman, a female version of the Hulk, a dragon lady, Dorothy of the Wizard of Oz or Alice in Wonderland. All of this research should recognize that we are human too, trying to do a difficult job in difficult circumstances with very little support or respect.[2]

All of this further underscores the need for women to help each other as we climb the walls, something that all of us Alphas now aspire to do. We need to give back and forward and lend a hand to the women coming up behind us so that their path is easier than ours was. At some level, all of us with our stories in this work have encountered some, if not all, of the paradoxes so aptly set out by Zheng.[2] I still contend that the third aspect of the bind, that of being underestimated and unwelcome is actually the biggest barrier and probably the biggest paradox of them all: being underestimated while ensuring we are exceptionally qualified. I'm not sure how to reconcile all of this, except to be aware of it, make your own rules and **Pound On!!**

The Queen Bee Phenomenon - Has she died off?

Along with women not helping each other generally, there is the issue of what top women leaders do for other women once they get to high level positions. I've already talked about the women who refused to help us in law firms, or help other women in the corporate world. Our Alpha experiences were a long time ago but the problem still persists. Some research indicates that the Queen Bee phenomenon has died off, but our experience, while limited, contradicts this. Let's first explore the phenomenon and what it means, and then explore whether the phenomenon still exists.

There is an assumption that there can be only one "Queen Bee" in an organization. She rises to the top, but guards her precarious position deftly not wanting other women to join her. Anne Welsh McNulty writes about this in her article in Harvard Business Review "Don't Underestimate the Power of Women Supporting Each Other at Work," where she talks about her career experiences at an investment bank[4]. McNulty recounts an experience where she tried to have lunch with the only woman senior to her, who turned down her invitation. Not only did the senior woman turn her down, she clearly told McNulty that they were not going "to be friends" as there was room for only one senior woman partner in the firm. Not too inviting, and still extremely common. This, says McNulty, is the Queen Bee phenomenon, where some senior women distance themselves from other more junior women. Perhaps this isolation is designed to make the Queen Bee more accepted by her male peers, she theorizes, or is an attempt by the Queen Bee to separate herself from a marginalized group[4]. By contrast, men are more likely (46%) to have an advocate of a higher rank (Sylvia Ann Hewlett is quoted in this regard).

The marginalization that McNulty experienced led her to isolate herself. Until other women started leaving the firm they didn't realize their common experience. Other women were having the same issues, but they weren't talking to each other about it. In the end, McNulty resolved never to let this happen to her again.

While other research casts doubt on the continued existence of the Queen Bee "Syndrome[5]", the stories of our Alphas suggest otherwise. Our other stories suggest that help from more senior women is a rare exception. I encountered a sole woman partner who was determined to sabotage the early in career women lawyers, and Lynda recounts similar stories. In fact, the poor treatment of women toward each other seems to begin in early childhood. Both Lynda and I recount stories of "mean girls" who were cruel to us. Lee talks about befriending a girl others had isolated. This lack of early role models for helping each other as girls followed us into the workplace decades later. It didn't stop when one woman succeeded; she still didn't want to help others.

Another question which arises in the research is whether there is an implicit quota for women at the top. In other words, once there is a Queen Bee, is the job of the organization done? Palmquist questions whether the presence of one top woman executive actually hinders the chances that another woman will get a similar appointment. He postulates that it's not the Queen Bee phenomenon alone in that women don't help each other, but that there's an implicit quota for top female executives. One woman might be invested in and promoted, he theorizes, in order to "put a face[5]" on gender diversity, but this limitation of women at the top preserves the status of the male-dominated power structure.

Palmquist refers to a study of women in senior positions at 1500 firms over a 20-year time frame. They found that the probability of a woman holding a leading role in a company is 51%

lower if there is another woman in the top management group. They call this "the negative spillover effect" i.e. appointing one woman at the top has a negative effect on the opportunities for other women in the firm. Some small "positive" spillover effects existed, but largely with respect to supporting professional roles, not to promotions to positions with higher levels of responsibility. In other words, any power is dispersed and doesn't change or threaten the company's fundamental power structure. They did find that the "CEO Queen Bee" brought in other women moreso than women further down in the organization.

Frankly, I still need to see the death and extinction of the Queen Bee to truly believe it. My experiences, and those of our Alphas, would suggest that she is still alive and well, quotas or not.

The Glass Ceiling and Other Glass Barriers

All my reading and research leads me to think that there are a lot of glass barriers in women's ways as we ascend the corporate ladder. I reference glass ceilings, glass cliffs, glass borders, glass staircases, escalators and labyrinths. I was struck by all of these so-called "invisible" barriers to our success, and began to wonder when we stopped chasing the handsome prince and the proverbial glass slipper, and started seeking our own "impeded" success instead.

When my daughter was a little girl I'd read her fairytales at night. The happy endings described a handsome prince, sometimes with a glass slipper in hand, rescuing the helpless girl and whisking her away to her happily ever after, likely on a white horse with her hair flying behind her. That, in a nutshell, was the fairytale. There was no dream of a great career equal to a man's, nor the ability to take care of ourselves throughout our lives. I always changed the endings of the nighttime stories. Instead of the handsome prince coming to the damsel's rescue I told my daughter: "Don't wait for a handsome prince. Get a good education, find a good job, and rescue yourself!!" I wanted her to be able to buy her own glass slippers. At the time, I was a young lawyer still climbing the walls. I was just starting to learn about all the invisible obstacles in my path. Hence the name of this book: "From the Glass Slipper to the Glass Ceiling". I wanted to share my rewritten fairytale, and describe what career pursuits are really like, both good and bad.

The Glass Ceiling is now a metaphor cemented into the common parlance of women and our careers. I still contend that we are not welcome in the first place, and that all these barriers, invisible and otherwise, are descriptions of mechanisms which protect existing power structures.

I do wish to state again, that this book is not meant as an academic treatise and is intended as a positive chronicle of women in attainable careers, sharing our lessons learned for other women to learn, especially those women coming up behind us. It is still important, however, to understand these "glass" concepts and barriers, especially as we collectively move to shatter them all.

The term the Glass Ceiling is attributed to Carol Hymowitz and Timothy Schellhardt of the Wall Street Journal. In 1986, when addressing the question of why there are so few women in the C-Suite[6] their answer was that women "could not break through the glass ceiling", meaning the invisible barrier between managerial positions and the C-Suite. (The concept was also outlined in the Corporate Woman, 1986, Kanter 1977 Morrison, White and Van Velsor 1987). While some previous opposition and constraints to women's careers had been legal in nature (see our timelines) opinions preventing women's advancement were loudly voiced even as late as the 1970s. Take former President Richard Nixon who would not consider appointing a woman to the United States Supreme Court[6] as he deemed women "erratic and emotional" moreso than men, and therefore considered women unsuited for "any government job whatsoever". (From the White House audio tapes made public through the Freedom of Information Act). With the most recent elected women in Congress he must be spinning in his grave.

Eagly & Carli contend that "times have changed"[6]. I'm not so sure about that. Times are different, but I'm not sure they've really changed all that much. While a few of us have made it into the C-Suite at corporations like me and Lee, others have formed our own companies and made our own C-Suites, like Cheryl and Lynda. What is absolutely certain is that we are subject to extreme scrutiny as we take these positions. I got comments that I was "under a microscope" as I took a C-level job. Male co-workers felt free to comment on everything from my clothing to my nail polish. Other Alphas were subjected to the same scrutiny, like Lynda, in law firms where she was objectified. Increased scrutiny of women is well-documented in the literature and in studies[7].

Let's take a closer look.

The Glass Cliff

While reading and researching women's career experiences, I came upon many articles which documented a disturbing phenomenon called "the Glass Cliff". It seems less well known than the Glass Ceiling concept, at least in non-academic circles, but may have unfortunate negative effects on future Alphas and their careers.

The concept of the Glass Cliff was first officially recognized by Michelle Ryan and Alex Haslam in 2005 and is cited in many subsequent works and articles, including much more recent ones[8]. The theory goes like this. Women encounter the invisible barrier of the Glass Ceiling and earn well-deserved senior leadership positions. However, many of these leadership positions are "precarious" in that they are inherently unstable. In other words, we are offered senior positions in organizations which are not doing well. Women are therefore destined to fail, and we create a self-fulfilling prophecy that women lack leadership capability even though their failure was inevitable. This cements the notion that women are not suited for C-Suite jobs even though they inherited precarious and unstable businesses which could not be fixed regardless of leadership gender[9]. The Glass Cliff also diminishes women's confidence and makes organizations reluctant to put women in executive positions.

Fraud syndrome, or imposter syndrome then becomes an issue with women in senior level jobs, a topic which we should further explore as well. Research conducted after Ryan and Haslam's work demonstrates that the Glass Cliff phenomenon is widespread and is not unique to any location or industry. Also disturbing is that most of such failures are internal hires who may have felt obligated to take on an "impossible" challenge[8].

None of these phenomena mean that we should shy away from opportunities. Quite the contrary. We should, however, take on tasks with our eyes wide open, and ask for coaching and support. Ongoing support and mentoring would help women succeed and make a lasting impact with reduced risk of negative career implications. To have real influence we need real power, and not just when times are bad[10].

The Leadership Labyrinth

In 2007, Eagly and Carli wrote about a concept which takes the glass ceiling barrier even further. Believing that the metaphor may be changing, they felt that the glass ceiling concept failed to capture the variety of complex challenges faced by women on our leadership journeys. They note that women disappear from leadership at many points along our climb to the glass ceiling. They feel that women face walls all around, or a labyrinth of barriers with various twists and turns along the way. While the "goal" might be attainable through various routes, some of the twists and turns are expected, and some are not. Among the obstacles faced, the authors name several, including vestiges of prejudice in that men earn more and are promoted faster than women, i.e. gender pay gaps exist where women earn approximately 81 cents for every dollar earned by men. Promotions come more slowly for women than for men, and this advantage grows for men throughout their careers. Gender bias has even been shown in essay evaluation, e.g. the Goldberg Paradigm in 1968 where names were changed on essays and male writers received higher grades than women for the same work[6].

Eagly and Carli found that the gender bias against women still exists at all levels, not just at the top, and that resistance to women's leadership continues. People associate men and women with different traits, and that more traits connoting leadership are associated with men than women i.e. agentic traits of aggression and assertion, rather than more communal traits which are more closely associated with women, i.e. compassion and caring. Similar to the double bind where women have to be tough and likable at the same time, these findings show that dominant behavior can be more damaging to women as these traits are not commonly associated with women. It is the same with self-promotion[6].

Demands of family life can also present twists and turns for women as we are more likely to interrupt our careers for family reasons. The bulk of domestic work still falls on women's shoulders. Women also have very little time for socializing with colleagues and building social networks. We Alphas all evaluated how to manage our careers and families. Some of us stepped away for a while, like me and Lynda, Cheryl hired a nanny, and Lee enjoyed her role as an aunt[6].

In the labyrinth of leadership there are many challenges for women along the way. The authors suggest that certain actions can help address the problems. They suggest, among other things, to increase awareness, change the long-hours norm, and ensure that women are in executive positions. Mentors and family-friendly policies will also help, especially welcoming women back who have taken leaves of absence[6].

In other words, look at the whole path and the maze to see solutions. That way, we can "stop the leaks in the lower floors of the building" and not just see the glass ceiling as the problem[6]. Hear hear.

CONCLUSIONS

I sat for a long time, trying to figure out what to say to close this book out. It's tough to let go of the idea that this creation is nearly done; I've worked on it for so long, and thought we all had so much to say. The more I wrote this book, the more I realized that there will always be more to learn, and more to say. Hence I need to conclude with a few parting words (until we meet again).

This book is partly an historical journey, and partly a forward-looking pathfinder. I thought it was important to look at where women have been, how far we've come, and how much work there is left to do. The Timelines showcase earlier times in our history, and the injustices women faced. They also show how far we have traveled, and the rights we are still looking to earn.

POUND ON

The Stories are heartfelt accounts from wonderful Alpha Women who generously poured out their life reflections and learnings. There are many positive lessons to learn, as well as poignant accounts of survival and challenges. Their stories of perseverance and tenacity are lessons for Alphas at all stages and phases of our journeys. Savor them and imagine their paths. Model your paths after whichever journeys most inspire you.

I was surprised and heartened at the things all of the Alphas have in common. Thus, the chapter on the Common Themes. We grew up in different places under different circumstances, but had some common elements to our lives and childhoods. We were really all born lucky, and capitalized on this luck with determination and hard work. We all feel truly blessed and are grateful for our lives so far.

The Concepts are meant to provide an overview, not an academic treatise. As I've said throughout, this work is not meant as a textbook or test case; it is accounts of positive stories of Alpha Women meant to inspire, motivate and help other Alphas pursue their dreams. Take the interview questions and use them. Ask other Alphas to share their stories. Continue to learn from them and understand their wisdom and how they earned it. So too with the Rules. Read mine, and make your own. Use the Rotenberg Axis to see where you are on your journey, and examine what you must do to attain the next level. Dream big and never give up. Above all else, be true to yourself and Pound On!! You can do this, I know you can.

POUND ON!!

EPILOGUE

As I write this, I am contemplating my next project, and where I can take my experience and Alpha knowledge next. I am hopeful that sharing these positive stories will truly inspire a next generation of Alpha Women, and give some hope and guidance along the way.

This will definitely NOT be my last book. It took my life so far to write this first one, but I intend to continue teaching and learning, sharing and listening, and giving back. There is always more to be done.

Stay tuned...

POUND ON

COMMENTS

From My Husband

When I first learned that my beautiful wife Robin was going to write a book about Alpha Women I thought that it would involve a new superhero aptly named Alpha Woman, who would fight evil and criminal elements with help from her sisters Wonder Woman, Super Woman and Bat Woman.

My imagination lit up with great expectations for future movie rights, cartoons, a clothing line, and toy figures all designed to establish and market the identity of this invulnerable character who could soothe the savage beast, while at the same time selectively destroy impediments that stand in her way.

After some research and thoughtful reflection I came to the realization that the concept of the Alpha had long been based upon the law of the jungle involving the survival of the fittest and control of the herd. In fact, Robin has long advised anyone who would listen that in our lives, we can either behave as sheep or leaders. Perhaps it was that view of life that ultimately gave rise to this book.

In truth, I never thought about my wife being either an Alpha, Beta or any other creature of the human jungle. Rather, it was her love, kindness and concern for others that helped to propel me towards her. I always knew that the drive, ambition and toughness was inside of her and would be unleashed at the appropriate time.

Ultimately, we are all shaped by our experiences and it is those seminal life events that make us into leaders, or sheep. Robin had the terrible misfortune of losing her mom at a very young age and it was that difficult challenge that likely made her the sweet, graceful, yet forceful survivor that I married.

Alpha is the first letter of the Greek alphabet and while being first is generally advisable, it is not meant for everyone. The more ancient and perhaps deeper meaning of Alpha is found in the Hebrew and Phoenician letter Aleph which means not merely a leader, but an ox. These incredible strong creatures toiled and worked hard to achieve their reputation as being indispensable. So perhaps Alpha Woman is a super hero. They toil in the fields of career, family and life in general, not as sheep, but leaders.

From My Daughter

One of my earliest memories is my mom telling me she loves me "more than anything". I got more "any's" as I got older, to make sure I got more than anybody else. Now I get 3 - she loves me more than "any any any thing".....Others may get 1 or 2, but she always makes sure I get the most. If my mom were an animal, she would be a swan. She is elegant and beautiful, serene and calm, at least above the surface. What you don't see is her paddling like mad underneath. And if you cross her or try to hurt me, she'll peck your head off. I always said, "You don't want to mess with my mom". I know she always has my back.

My mom is the strongest woman I know. No matter what is going on, I know she will hold her head high and keep going. She would do anything to help me and my son Carter. I'm really proud and happy that she wrote this book to tell her amazing story, and the stories of her friends and colleagues. She has achieved a lot in the corporate world, but worked really hard when I was growing up to take care of me and build her career at the same time. Her jobs were tough, and she didn't have much help. I really don't know how she did it all. I don't know where I would be without my mom. I love you mamas. More than anything. Love Taryn. xo

ACKNOWLEDGMENTS

First and foremost, I'd like to thank my family. While their initial skepticism was palpable, they came around to the idea that I might have something valuable to contribute to the women coming up behind me. They do keep me grounded, and definitely keep my head from swelling.

To be more specific:

To the love of my life - my husband Mitch - You are my destiny, my ultimate partner, my true and complete love. Always and forever.

To my beautiful daughter Taryn - You are my dream come true, an answered prayer, and my over the rainbow.

To my sweet Grandson Carter, who has no idea that I've ever written anything other than his name in letters on the fridge - words cannot express the joy and happiness you bring to my life. The mere thought of you melts my heart and fills me with gratitude.

To my Mother and Grandmothers who watch over me. You taught me how to live, love and persevere. I try to honor you every day and hope I make you proud.

To all my Alphas - my deepest appreciation for opening your hearts, embracing this project and sharing your amazing journeys so far. You spent many hours writing and telling your stories to complete your chapters. You have my total respect and admiration.

This work was inspired by my good friend and colleague Cris Brito, a native of Brazil, who is the consummate Alpha Woman. She generously coached and coaxed me into the idea of writing this book. I am grateful for her creativity and support.

Acknowledgments

This book would not have been possible without my Project Manager Marilyn Brady who from the start has tolerated my many changes and somewhat crazy ideas. I am eternally grateful to Rebecca Best of Emineo Marketing who used her great skill, ability and patience to bring my brand to life with her brilliant marketing ideas and creativity. My editor Meg Fry was instrumental in perfecting the Alpha Stories, making them more readable. Special thanks to the Groton Teacher Stacey Spring and her students who helped edit and footnote the Timelines.

Thanks also to my extended family and friends for their enthusiasm, support and encouragement.

POUND ON

A

ENDNOTES: TIMELINE OF WOMEN'S RIGHTS UNITED STATES OF AMERICA

1. Lewis, Jone Johnson. "The Blackstone Commentaries and Women's Rights." ThoughtCo, Feb. 11, 2020, thoughtco.com/blackstone-commentaries-profile-3525208.

2. Sir William Blackstone, Commentaries on the Laws of England, Book the First: Chapter the Fifteenth: Of Husband and Wife. 4 vols. Oxford: Printed at the New-York Historical Society Clarendon Press, 1765–1769.

3. "Timeline for Women's Rights." Topic Timeline, Digital History, 2019, www.digitalhistory.uh.edu/timelines/timelinetopics.cfm?tltopicid=3.

4. The Editors of Encyclopedia Britannica. "Married Women's Property Acts." Encyclopedia Britannica, Encyclopedia Britannica, Inc., 8 Sept. 2010, www.britannica.com/event/Married-Womens-Property-Acts-United-States-1839.

5. The Editors of Encyclopedia Britannica. "Seneca Falls Convention." Encyclopedia Britannica, Encyclopdia Britannica, Inc., 7 Feb. 2020, www.britannica.com/event/Seneca-Falls-Convention.

6. The Editors of Encyclopedia Britannica. "Fourteenth Amendment." Encyclopedia Britannica, Encycloedia Britannica, Inc., 27 Sept. 2019, www.britannica.com/topic/Fourteenth-Amendment.

7. The Editors of Encyclopedia Britannica. "Arabella Mansfield." Encyclopedia Britannica, Encyclopedia Britannica, Inc., 29 July 2019, www.britannica.com/biography/Arabella-Mansfield.

8. The Editors of Encyclopedia Britannica. "Women's Suffrage." Encyclopedia Britannica, Encyclopedia Britannica, Inc., 24 Mar. 2020, www.britannica.com/topic/woman-suffrage.

9. "Timeline for Women's Rights." Digital History, 2019, www.digitalhistory.uh.edu/timelines/timelinetopics.cfm?tltopicid=3.

10. "Timeline for Women's Rights." Digital History, 2019, www.digitalhistory.uh.edu/timelines/timelinetopics.cfm?tltopicid=3.

11. Linder, Douglas. "The trial of Susan B. Anthony for Illegal Voting" http//IJURIST.LAW.PITT.EDU/TRIALS14.HTM (2001)

12. "Timeline for Women's Rights." Digital History, 2019, www.digitalhistory.uh.edu/timelines/timelinetopics.cfm?tltopicid=3.

13. "Timeline for Women's Rights." Digital History, 2019, www.digitalhistory.uh.edu/timelines/timelinetopics.cfm?tltopicid=3.

14. "Susanna Madora Salter." Emily Taylor Center for Women & Gender Equity, University of Kansas, 22 May 2013, emilytaylorcenter.ku.edu/pioneer-woman/salter.

15. Milligan, Susan. "Stepping Through History." U.S. News & World Report, U.S. News & World Report, 20 Jan. 2017, www.usnews.com/news/the-report/articles/2017-01-20/timeline-the-womens-rights-movement-in-the-us.

16. National Constitution Center - Centuries of Citizenship - Map: States Grant Women the Right to Vote, constitutioncenter.org/timeline/html/cw08_12159.html.

17. Milligan, Susan. "Stepping Through History." U.S. News & World Report, U.S. News & World Report, 20 Jan. 2017, www.usnews.com/news/the-report/articles/2017-01-20/timeline-the-womens-rights-movement-in-the-us.

18. Milligan, Susan. "Stepping Through History." U.S. News & World Report, U.S. News & World Report, 20 Jan. 2017, www.usnews.com/news/the-report/articles/2017-01-20/timeline-the-womens-rights-movement-in-the-us.

19. "Birth Control Organizations." The Margaret Sanger Papers Project, MSPP / About Sanger / Birth Control Organizations, www.nyu.edu/projects/sanger/aboutms/organization_ppfa.php.

20. Joint Resolution of Congress proposing a constitutional amendment extending the right of suffrage to women, approved June 4, 1919.; Ratified Amendments, 1795-1992; General Records of the United States Government; Record Group 11; National Archives.

21. "Women's Rights Movement." National Women's History Alliance, The National Women's History Alliance and Endorsed by National and State Organizations, nationalwomenshistoryalliance.org/resources/womens-rights-movement/.

22. "Women in the United States Senate." Wikipedia, Wikimedia Foundation, 2 May 2020, en.wikipedia.org/wiki/Women_in_the_United_States_Senate.

23. Breitman, Jessica. "Honoring the Achievements of FDR's Secretary of Labor." FDR Presidential Library and Museum, www.fdrlibrary.org/perkins.

24. "Lettie Pate Evans ." Lettie Pate Evans Foundation, lpevans.org/about/lettie-pate-evans/.

25. Sanger, Margaret. "The Status of Birth Control: 1938." The New Republic, The New Republic Magazine, 20 Apr. 1938, newrepublic.com/article/100850/the-status-birth-control-1938.

26. "The FDA Approves the Pill." PBS, Public Broadcasting Service, www.pbs.org/wgbh/americanexperience/features/pill-us-food-and-drug-administration-approves-pill/.

27. Jewish Women's Archive. "Publication of "The Feminine Mystique" by Betty Friedan." , https://jwa.org/thisweek/feb/17/1963/betty-friedan

28. "The Equal Pay Act of 1963." U.S. Equal Employment Opportunity Commission, www.eeoc.gov/statutes/equal-pay-act-1963.

29. "The Civil Rights Act of 1964." Constitutional Rights Foundation, www.crf-usa.org/black-history-month/the-civil-rights-act-of-1964.

30. "Title VII of the Civil Rights Act of 1964." U.S. Equal Employment Opportunity Commission, www.eeoc.gov/laws/statutes/titlevii.cfm.

31. "Timeline of Important EEOC Events." U.S. Equal Employment Opportunity Commission, www.eeoc.gov/youth/timeline-important-eeoc-events.

32. "History of the Abortion Debate." NPR.org, National Public Radio (NPR), www.npr.org/news/specials/roevwade/timeline.html.

33. "Timeline of Important EEOC Events." U.S. Equal Employment Opportunity Commission, www.eeoc.gov/youth/timeline-important-eeoc-events.

34. Wilcox, W. Bradford. "The Evolution of Divorce." National Affairs, 2009, nationalaffairs.com/publications/detail/the-evolution-of-divorce.

35. Michals, Debra, PhD. "Shirley Chisholm." National Women's History Museum, 2015, www.womenshistory.org/education-resources/biographies/shirley-chisholm.

36. "Phillips v. Martin Marietta Corporation." Oyez, www.oyez.org/cases/1970/73.

37. "ERA History." EqualRightsAmendment.org, www equalrightsamendment.org/history.

38. "The Civil Rights Act of 1964 and the Equal Employment Opportunity Commission". National Archives. 2016-08-15. Archived from the original on 2017-10-20.

39. "Eisenstadt v. Baird, 405 U.S. 438 (1972)." Justia Law, supreme.justia.com/cases/federal/us/405/438/.

40. The Editors of Encyclopedia Britannica. "Juanita Morris Kreps." Encyclopedia Britannica, Encyclopedia Britannica, Inc., 7 Jan. 2020, www.britannica.com/biography/Juanita-Morris-Kreps.

41. "Roe v. Wade." Oyez, www.oyez.org/cases/1971/70-18.

42. "Fair Housing Act and Amendments." www.nolo.com, 20 June 2012, www.nolo.com/legal-encyclopedia/content/fair-housing-act.html.

43. "The Fair Housing Act." The United States Department of Justice, 21 Dec. 2017, www.justice.gov/crt/fair-housing-act-1#sex.

44. "Cleveland Board of Education v. LaFleur." Oyez, www.oyez.org/cases/1973/72-777.

45. "A Reflection on the History of Sexual Assault Laws in the United States." The Arkansas Journal of Social Change and Public Service, 20 Apr. 2019, ualr.edu/socialchange/2018/04/15/reflection-history-sexual-assault-laws-united-states/.

46. "The Pregnancy Discrimination Act of 1978." U.S. Equal Employment Opportunity Commission, www.eeoc.gov/statutes/pregnancy-discrimination-act-1978.

47. "Paula Fickes Hawkins," in Women in Congress, 1917-2006. Prepared under the direction of the Committee on House Administration by the Office of History & Preservation, U.S. House of Representatives. Washington, D.C.: Government Printing Office, 2006.

48. "Women in the Senate." Senate.gov, United States Senate, 27 Jan. 2020, www.senate.gov/artandhistory/history/common/briefing/women_senators.htm.

49. Smentkowski, Brian P. "Sandra Day O'Connor." Encyclopedia Britannica, Encyclopedia Britannica, Inc., 22 Mar. 2020, www.britannica.com/biography/Sandra-Day-OConnor.

50. Anderson, Ashlee. Sally Ride. 16 Aug. 2018, www.womenshistory.org/education-resources/biographies/sally-ride.

51. “Geraldine Anne Ferraro.” US House of Representatives: History, Art & Archives, U.S. House of Representatives, history.house.gov/People/Detail/13081.

52. Dagley, David L. “Meritor Savings Bank v. Vinson.” Encyclopedia Britannica, Encyclopedia Britannica, Inc., 9 Jan. 2020, www.britannica.com/topic/Meritor-Savings-Bank-v-Vinson.

53. “The Year of the Woman, 1992: US House of Representatives: History, Art & Archives.” Year of the Woman, 1992 | US House of Representatives: History, Art & Archives, history.house.gov/Exhibitions-and-Publications/WIC/Historical-Essays/Assembling-Amplifying-Ascending/Women-Decade/.

54. Tikkanen, Amy. “Anita Hill.” Encyclopedia Britannica, Encyclopedia Britannica, Inc., 12 Apr. 2019, www.britannica.com/biography/Anita-Hill.

55. “Violence Against Women Act of 1993 (S.11 - 103rd Congress (1993-1994)).” Congress.gov, www.congress.gov/bill/103rd-congress/senate-bill/11.

56. “United States v. Virginia.” Oyez, www.oyez.org/cases/1995/94-1941.

57. The Editors of Encyclopaedia Britannica. “Madeleine Albright.” Encyclopedia Britannica, Encyclopedia Britannica, Inc., 23 Apr. 2020, www.britannica.com/biography/Madeleine-Albright.

58. Norwood, Arlisha. “Condoleezza Rice.” National Women’s History Museum. National Women’s History Museum, 2017.

59. The Editors of Encyclopedia Britannica. "Nancy Pelosi." Encyclopedia Britannica, Encyclopedia Britannica, Inc., 22 Mar. 2020, www.britannica.com/biography/Nancy-Pelosi.

60. The Editors of Encyclopaedia Britannica. "Sarah Palin." Encyclopædia Britannica, Encyclopædia Britannica, Inc., 7 Feb. 2020, www.britannica.com/biography/Sarah-Heath-Palin.

61. Londoño, Ernesto. "Pentagon Removes Ban on Women in Combat." The Washington Post, WP Company, 24 Jan. 2013, www.washingtonpost.com/world/national-security/pentagon-to-remove-ban-on-women-in-combat/2013/01/23/6cba86f6-659e-11e2-85f5-a8a9228e55e7_story.html?utm_term=471c91c2a526.

62. Patrick, Jeanette. "Hillary Rodham Clinton." National Women's History Museum. National Women's History Museum, 2016.

63. "Women in the United States Army." The United States Army, www.army.mil/women/history/.

64. Dailey, Daniel A., et al. "U.S. Army." U.S. Army, https://www.army.mil/e2/downloads/rv7/women/full_integration_of_women_in_the_army.pdf.

65. "Women in U.S. Congress 2017." Center for American Women and Politics, Rutgers Eagleton Institute of Politics, 8 Feb. 2018, cawp.rutgers.edu/women-us-congress-2017.

66. Sheth, Sonam. "More than 3 Million People Believed to Have Protested on the Day after Trump's Inauguration." Business Insider, Business Insider, 25 Jan. 2017, www.businessinsider.com/more-than-3-million-people-marched-on-saturday-for-the-womens-march-2017-1.

ENDNOTES: TIMELINE OF WOMEN'S RIGHTS CANADA

1. "Canadian History of Women's Rights." The Nellie McClung Foundation, www.ournellie.com/learn/womens-suffrage/canadian-history-of-womens-rights/.

2. "Harriet Tubman and Women's Rights." Harriet Tubman

   Historical Society, www.harriet-tubman.org/women-rights-suffrage/.

3. "Mary Ann Shadd." Wikipedia, Wikimedia Foundation, 21

   Apr. 2020, en.wikipedia.org/wiki/Mary_Ann_Shadd.

4. Specia, Megan. "Overlooked No More: How Mary Ann Shadd Cary Shook Up the Abolitionist Movement." The New York Times, The New York Times, 6 June 2018, www.nytimes.com/2018/06/06/obituaries/mary-ann-shadd-cary-abolitionist-overlooked.html.

5. "Canadian History of Women's Rights." The Nellie McClung Foundation, www.ournellie.com/learn/womens-suffrage/canadian-history-of-womens-rights/.

6. "Canadian History of Women's Rights." The Nellie McClung Foundation, www.ournellie.com/learn/womens-suffrage/canadian-history-of-womens-rights/.

7. "Canadian History of Women's Rights." The Nellie McClung Foundation, www.ournellie.com/learn/womens-suffrage/canadian-history-of-womens-rights/.
8. "Timeline: Status of Canadian Women." Osstftoronta.ca, 21 June 2013, osstftoronto/ca/wp-content/uploads/2013/11/Womans-Timeline.pdf.

9. Blackhouse, Constance. "MARTIN, CLARA BRETT." Dictionary of Canadian Biography, Vol. 15, University of Toronto/Université Laval, 2005, www.biographi.ca/en/bio/martin_clara_brett_15E.html.

10. Blackwell, John D.. "Clara Brett Martin". The Canadian Encyclopedia, 04 March 2015, Historica Canada. https://www.thecanadianencyclopedia.ca/en/article/clara-brett-martin. .

11. Smirle, Corinne. "Emma Sophia Baker." Psychology's Feminist Voices, 2012, www.feministvoices.com/emma-sophia-baker/.

12. "A History of Canadian Sexual Assault Legislation 1900-2000." Constance Backhouse: Abduction of an Heiress, www.constancebackhouse.ca/fileadmin/website/abducth.htm.

13. MacGregor, Mary. "Proving a Rustling Charge." Proving

a Rustling Charge, Beef in B.C., 1989, 2006, www.marymacgregor.ca/article40.htm.

14. "A History of Canadian Sexual Assault Legislation 1900-2000." Constance Backhouse, www.constancebackhouse.ca/fileadmin/website/1909.htm.

15. Strong-Boag, Veronica. "Women's Suffrage in Canada". The Canadian Encyclopedia, 25 August 2016, Historica Canada. https://www.thecanadianencyclopedia.ca/en/article/suffrage.

16. "Women's Suffrage in Saskatchewan." Women's Suffrage in Saskatchewan | Provincial Archives of Saskatchewan, 2011, www.saskarchives.com/Suffrage.

17. Strong-Boag, Veronica. "Women's Suffrage in Canada". The

Canadian Encyclopedia, 25 August 2016, Historica Canada. https://www.thecanadianencyclopedia.ca/en/article/suffrage. Accessed 06 May 2020.

18. Pettinger, Tejvan. "Biography of Emily Murphy", Oxford, www.biographyonline.net Published 1 February 2010. Last updated: 12 February 2018.

19. Culbertson, Debbie. "Roberta MacAdams Price". The Canadian Encyclopedia, 31 March 2015, Historica Canada. https://www.thecanadianencyclopedia.ca/en/article/roberta-macadams-price

20. "The Evolution of the Federal Franchise." Elections Canada, Dec. 2014, www.elections.ca/content.aspx?section=vot&dir=bkg&:document=ec90785&lang=e.

21. "Women's Suffrage in Atlantic Canada." The Canadian Encyclopedia, Historica Canada, www.thecanadianencyclopedia.ca/en/timeline/womens-suffrage-in-atlantic-canada.

22. Kelly, Paula. "Looking for Mrs. Armstrong." Canada's History, 9 Jan. 2016, www.canadashistory.ca/explore/women/looking-for-mrs-armstrong.

23. Reilly, J. Nolan. "Winnipeg General Strike of 1919". The

Canadian Encyclopedia, 07 October 2019, Historica Canada. https://www.thecanadianencyclopedia.ca/en/article/winnipeg-general-strike.

24. Hallett, Mary E.. "Nellie McClung". The Canadian Encyclopedia, 03 October 2018, Historica Canada. https://www.thecanadianencyclopedia.ca/en/article/nellie-letitia-mcclung.

25. "Social Justice Reform for the Benefit of Women in British Columbia." Legislative Assembly of British Columbia, Legislative Assembly of British Columbia, www.leg.bc.ca/content-peo/Learning-Resources/WHM-2015-Part-2-Social-Justice-Reform-English.pdf.

26. Klowak, Sandy. "History Idol: Agnes Macphail." Canada's History, 30 Sept. 2010, www.canadashistory.ca/explore/women/history-idol-agnes-macphail.

27. Marshall, Tabitha. "Agnes Macphail". The Canadian Encyclopedia, 28 August 2015, Historica Canada. https://www.thecanadianencyclopedia.ca/en/article/agnes-macphail.

28. "Significant Dates in History of Women." Prince Edward Island Women in Government, PEI Coalition for Women In Government, 2010, www.peiwomeningovernment.ca/significant-dates-in-history.

29. "Divorces in Canada, 1925." Published by Authority of the Hon. J. A. Robb, M. P., Acting Miniter of Trade and Commerce, 1925.

30. Cavanaugh, Catherine and Susanna McLeod. "Irene Parlby". The Canadian Encyclopedia, 03 October 2018, Historica Canada. https://www.thecanadianencyclopedia.ca/en/article/mary-irene-parlby. Accessed 06 May 2020.

31. "Canadian Women's 150: 150 Years of Canadian Women's Accomplishments." Make It Our Business, Western Center for Research and Education on Violence Against Women, 28 June 2017, makeitourbusiness.ca/blog/canadian-womens-150-150-years-canadian-womens-accomplishments.

32. Marshall, Tabitha and David A. Cruickshank. "Persons Case". The Canadian Encyclopedia, 18 October 2019, Historica Canada. https://www.thecanadianencyclopedia.ca/en/article/persons-case.

33. Marshall, Tabitha and David A. Cruickshank. "Persons Case". The Canadian Encyclopedia, 18 October 2019, Historica Canada. https://www.thecanadianencyclopedia.ca/en/article/persons-case.

34. "INTERNATIONAL WOMEN'S DAY." Canadian Labour Institute, Canadian Foundation for Labour Rights, 14 Mar. 2018, www.canadianlabourinstitute.org/story/international-women%27s-day.

35. Strong-Boag, Veronica. "Women's Suffrage in Canada". The Canadian Encyclopedia, 25 August 2016, Historica Canada. https://www.thecanadianencyclopedia.ca/en/article/suffrage.

36. Ramkhalawansingh, Ceta. "Know Your History on Pay Equity." Policy Options, 11 Apr. 2017, policyoptions.irpp.org/magazines/april-2017/know-your-history-on-pay-equity/.

37. Williams, Patricia. "Ellen Fairclough". The Canadian Encyclopedia, 16 December 2013, Historica Canada. https://www.thecanadianencyclopedia.ca/en/article/ellen-fairclough.

38. "Women & The Right To Vote In Canada: An Important Clarification." CBCnews, CBC/Radio Canada, www.cbc.ca/strombo/news/women-the-right-to-vote-in-canada-an-important-clarification.html.

39. "Le Code Civil De Quebec." BibliotheQue, http://www.bibliotheque.assnat.qc.ca/guides/fr/le-code-civil-du-bas-canada-a-aujourd-hui/342-1964-bill-16?ref=93

40. "Birth-Control Pill Turns 50." CBCnews, The Canadian Press, 10 May 2010, www.cbc.ca/news/birth-control-pill-turns-50-1.908892.

41. "Abortion in Canada." Abortion in Canada | The Canadian Encyclopedia, www.thecanadianencyclopedia.ca/en/article/abortion.

42. "Unemployment Insurance Fund Gets Richer in 1971 - CBC Archives." CBCnews, CBC/Radio Canada, www.cbc.ca/archives/entry/employment-insurance-ui-gets-richer-in-1971.

43. Ito, Gail Arlene. "Rosemary Brown (1930-2003)." Welcome to Blackpast •, 20 Aug. 2019, www.blackpast.org/global-african-history/brown-rosemary-1930-2003/.

44. "Pauline Jewett Institute of Women's and Gender Studies." Women's and Gender Studies, The Pauline Jewett Institute, carleton.ca/womensstudies/about-us/pauline-jewett-bio/.

45. Macleod, R.C.. "Royal Canadian Mounted Police (RCMP)".

The Canadian Encyclopedia, 15 November 2016, Historica Canada. https://www.thecanadianencyclopedia.ca/en/article/royal-canadian-mounted-police.

46. https:/vancouverisland.ctv.news.ca/vancouver-island-features/i-just-forged-ahead-the-story-of-one-of-canada-s-first-female-rcmp-officers-1.4277849

47. Anderssen, Erin. "No Memoirs for McDonough Yet." The Globe and Mail, 6 June 2002, www.theglobeandmail.com/news/national/no-memoirs-for-mcdonough-yet/article4135982/.

48. The Editors of Encyclopaedia Britannica. "Jeanne Mathilde Sauvé." Encyclopædia Britannica, Encyclopædia Britannica, Inc., 22 Apr. 2020, www.britannica.com/biography/Jeanne-Mathilde-Sauve.

49. Legislative Services Branch. "Consolidated Federal Laws of Canada, Access to Information Act." Legislative Services Branch, 1 May 2020, laws-lois.justice.gc.ca/eng/const/page-15.html.

50. The Editors of Encyclopaedia Britannica. "Bertha Wilson." Encyclopædia Britannica, Encyclopædia Britannica, Inc., 24 Apr. 2020, www.britannica.com/biography/Bertha-Wilson.

51. "Bertha Wilson." Bertha Wilson | The Canadian Encyclopedia, www.thecanadianencyclopedia.ca/en/article/bertha-wilson.

52. Alphonso, Caroline, and Marjan Farahbaksh. "Canadian Law Only Changed 26 Years Ago." The Globe and Mail, 1 Apr. 2009, www.theglobeandmail.com/news/world/canadian-law-only-changed-26-years-ago/article1150644/.

53. "Sexual Harassment Persists in Canada." Sexual Harassment Persists in Canada | Canadian Human Rights Commission, www.chrc-ccdp.gc.ca/eng/content/sexual-harassment-persists-canada.

54. Tremblay, Jean-noel. "Jeanne Sauvé". The Canadian Encyclopedia, 26 February 2018, Historica Canada. https://www.thecanadianencyclopedia.ca/en/article/jeanne-mathilde-sauve.

55. "Bill C-31." Indigenousfoundations, indigenousfoundations.arts.ubc.ca/bill_c-31/.

56. "Abortion Rights: Significant Moments in Canadian History | CBC News." CBCnews, CBC/Radio Canada, 27 Mar. 2017, www.cbc.ca/news/canada/abortion-rights-significant-moments-in-canadian-history-1.787212.

57. "1989: Audrey McLaughlin Becomes First Woman to Lead a National Party - CBC Archives." CBCnews, CBC/Radio Canada, www.cbc.ca/archives/entry/1989-audrey-mclaughlin-is-first-woman-to-lead-a-national-party.

58. National Defence. "Women in the Canadian Armed Forces." Backgrounder, 14 Aug. 2018, www.forces.gc.ca/en/news/article.page?doc=women-in-the-canadian-armed-forces/hie8w7rm.

59. The Editors of Encyclopaedia Britannica. "Kim Campbell." Encyclopædia Britannica, Encyclopædia Britannica, Inc., 6 Mar. 2020, www.britannica.com/biography/Kim-Campbell.

60. Calhoun, David. "Beverley McLachlin." Encyclopædia Britannica, Encyclopædia Britannica, Inc., 3 Sept. 2019, www.britannica.com/biography/Beverley-McLachlin.

61. "Louise Charron." Supreme Court of Canada, 4 Nov. 2011, www.scc-csc.ca/judges-juges/bio-eng.aspx?id=louise-charron.

62. Abella, Irving. "Rosalie Silberman Abella." Jewish Women's Archive, jwa.org/encyclopedia/article/abella-rosalie-silberman.

63. "Rosalie Silberman Abella." Supreme Court of Canada, 18 Mar. 2019, www.scc-csc.ca/judges-juges/bio-eng.aspx?id=rosalie-silberman-abella.

64. "Her Excellency the Right Honourable Michaëlle Jean, LL.D." University of Manitoba, 5 June 2007, umanitoba.ca/admin/governance/senate/hdr/848.html.

65. Martin, Michel. "Michaelle Jean: Canada's First Black Head Of State." NPR, 2 Apr. 2009.

66. Senate. "Senator Bev Busson." Senate of Canada, sencanada.ca/en/senators/busson-bev.

67. "Ontario New Democratic Party." GENi, www.geni.com/projects/Ontario-New-Democratic-Party/31378.

68. "Dunderdale Becomes 1st Woman to Lead N.L. | CBC News." CBCnews, CBC/Radio Canada, 3 Dec. 2010, www.cbc.ca/news/canada/newfoundland-labrador/dunderdale-becomes-1st-woman-to-lead-n-1-1.959039.

69. "Kathleen O. Wynne." Legislative Assembly of Ontario, www.ola.org/en/members/all/kathleen-o-wynne.

70. Leslie, Keith. "Parents Tell Kathleen Wynne Having Openly Gay Premier Makes Their Homosexual Kids Safer." CBCnews, CBC/Radio Canada, 9 Apr. 2015, www.cbc.ca/news/canada/kitchener-waterloo/parents-tell-kathleen-wynne-having-openly-gay-premier-makes-their-homosexual-kids-safer-1.3025842.

71. Munn-Rivard, Laura. "Women in Canada's Parliament." HillNotes, 4 Nov. 2015, hillnotes.ca/2015/11/04/women-in-canadas-parliament-making-progress-2/.

72. Murphy, Jessica. "Trudeau Gives Canada First Cabinet with Equal Number of Men and Women." The Guardian, Guardian News and Media, 4 Nov. 2015, www.theguardian.com/world/2015/nov/04/canada-cabinet-gender-diversity-justin-trudeau.

73. "Employment Standards." Government of Saskatchewan, www.saskatchewan.ca/business/employment-standards/vacations-holidays-leaves-and-absences/leaves-family-medical-and-service/interpersonal-violence-leave.

74. Przybyla, Heidi M., and Fredreka Schouten. "At 2.6 Million Strong, Women's Marches Crush Expectations." USA Today, Gannett Satellite Information Network, 22 Jan. 2017, www.usatoday.com/story/news/politics/2017/01/21/womens-march-aims-start-movement-trump-inauguration/96864158.

POUND ON

ENDNOTES: CONCEPTS

1. Locker, Melissa. "Women Need Other Women to Get Ahead in the Workplace, Says Science." Fast Company, Fast Company, 28 Jan. 2019, www.fastcompany.com/90297884/women-need-other-women-to-get-ahead-in-the-workplace-says-science.

2. Zheng, Wei, et al. "How Women Manage the Gendered Norms of Leadership." Harvard Business Review, 22 Nov. 2019, hbr.org/2018/11/how-women-manage-the-gendered-norms-of-leadership.

3. Bazelon, Emily. "Why Aren't Women Advancing More in Corporate America?" The New York Times, The New York Times, 21 Feb. 2019, www.nytimes.com/interactive/2019/02/21/magazine/women-corporate-america.html.

4. McNulty, Anne Welsh, et al. "Don't Underestimate the Power of Women Supporting Each Other at Work." Harvard Business Review, 3 Sept. 2018, hbr.org/2018/09/dont-underestimate-the-power-of-women-supporting-each-other-at-work.

5. Palmquist, Matt. "Why Are There So Few Women in the C-Suite?" Strategy Business, 17 Mar. 2016, www.strategy-business.com/blog/Why-Are-There-So-Few-Women-in-the-C-Suite?gko=9629d.

6. Eagly, Alice and Carli, L.L. Women and the Labyrinth of Leadership. Sept. 2007. Career Planning p. 2, 4, 5, 6-8 12, 16-20

7. (Early, Karau, Makhijani, 1995 as quoted in Ryan, Michelle, K, and Haslam, S. Alexander. The Glass Cliff: Evidence that women are over-represented in precarious leadership positions. British Journal of Management. Vol. 16, pp. 81-90 (2005))

8. Whawell, Susanna. “Women Are Shattering the Glass Ceiling Only to Fall off the Glass Cliff.” The Conversation, 18 Feb. 2020, theconversation.com/women-are-shattering-the-glass-ceiling-only-to-fall-off-the-glass-cliff-94071.

9. Murrell, Audrey. “The New Wave Of Women Leaders: Breaking The Glass Ceiling Or Facing The Glass Cliff?” Forbes, Forbes Magazine, 9 Jan. 2019, www.forbes.com/sites/audreymurrell/2018/12/03/the-new-wave-of-women-leaders-breaking-the-glass-ceiling-or-facing-the-glass-cliff/#78d6d5431ddb.

10. Palmquist, Matt. “Female Directors and Their Impact on Strategic Change.” Strategy Business, Harvard Business Review, 12 May 2014, www.strategy-business.com/blog/Female-Directors-and-Their-Impact-on-Strategic-Change?gko=e73b4.